Under The Sign Of The Big Fiddle

Under The Sign Of The Big Fiddle

The R.S. Williams Family
Manufacturers and Collectors
of Musical Instruments

Ladislav Cselenyi-Granch

Natural Heritage/Natural History Inc.

Copyright © 1996 by Ladislav Cselenyi-Granch All rights reserved. No portion of this book, with the exception of brief extracts for the purpose of literary or scholarly review, may be reproduced in any form without the permission of the publisher.

Published by Natural Heritage/Natural History Inc.
P.O. Box 95, Station O, Toronto, Ontario M4A 2M8

Canadian Cataloguing in Publication Data
1920 – Cselenyi-Granch, Ladislav
Under the Sign of The Big Fiddle
Includes bibliographical, appendix references and index.
ISBN 1-896219-17-9
1. Ontario - Manufacturing - 19th century.
2. Ontario - Music - 19th century.

Design by Derek Chung Tiam Fook

Natural Heritage / Natural History Inc. acknowledges with gratitude the assistance of the Canada Council, the Ontario Arts Council and the Association for the Export of Canadian Books

Printed and bound in Canada by
Hignell Printing Limited, Winnipeg, Manitoba

Front Cover
R.S. Williams (top hat) and factory workers in 1863, James Coleman and his son are second and sixth from the right, with what may be the first Victoria organ made by R.S. Williams. Courtesy Mrs. I.W. Brock, b. Williams.

Inside Front Cover
Advertising Leaflet of Williams Piano Patrons. Courtesy Metropolitan Toronto Library Board.

Inside Back Cover
Page 208 from the R.S. Williams Catalogue, No. 36, 1918. Courtesy National Library of Canada.

Outside Back Cover
The founder and president, and the vice president, as shown in Catalogue, No. 31. Courtesy Music Division, National Library of Canada, Ottawa.

Dedicated to my wife Judith with love.

TABLE OF CONTENTS

Acknowledgments 8
Preface 9

1. **Richard Sugden Williams: The Early Years (1834 - 1856)** 10
   Immigration and settlement of the Williams family in Ontario; R.S. Williams' school years; the path to an unexpected profession.

2. **Starting Out Under the Big Fiddle (1856-1864)** 15
   Toronto's musical climate; establishment of the new firm; early achievements.

3. **R.S. Williams and the Free-Reed Organ (1864-1870)** 22
   The Victoria Organ; the struggle for new goals.

4. **The Piano Industry (1872-1880)** . . . 32
   The eve of R.S. Williams' piano manufacture; the Canada Organ & Piano Company; the family business, R.S. Williams & Son.

5. **One Thousand Pianos Per Year (1880-1887)** 41
   Williams pianos on the North American piano market; introduction of R.S. Williams Jr., to the business.

6. **The Family Business Expands (1888-1899)** 49
   Relocation of the piano production to the Oshawa plant; Richard Sugden Williams Jr., as vice-president of the business; the venture into pipe-organ manufacturing.

7. **The Turn of the Century (1890-1906)** 61
   The publication of sheet music, a sideline; the family firm divided into Williams Piano Company Ltd. and R.S. Williams & Sons Co. Ltd.; the death of the founder.

8. **R.S. Williams Jr., as Collector (1905-1915)** 71
   Unique catalogues of rare violins and old musical instruments; the new president as collector and violin expert.

9. **A Great Gift to Toronto and Canada (1902-1916)** 82
   The New Scale Williams Piano; the opening of the Williams Music House; the donation of the collection to the Royal Ontario Museum.

10. **The Last Decades of the Firm (1914-1931)** 92
    The Edison phonograph; the war years; the violins of Auguste Delivet; seventy-five years of musical service.

11. **A World of Music History (1927-1945)** 104
    R.S. Williams Jr. – connoisseur, collector, and music lover to the very end.

Epilogue 111
Appendix A:
   Patents for Piano Improvements and Attachments 113
Appendix B:
   Toronto Director Listings for 1892 . . . 115
Appendix C: *Organ Specifications* 117
Appendix D:
   The Publication of Sheet Music Notes
   119
Endnotes 124
Index 132
About the Author 136

ACKNOWLEDGMENTS

My grateful thanks go first to the Royal Ontario Museum for permission to use the Museum's collections in my research and for the photographic documentation in this book.

I am greatly indebted to all members of R.S. Williams' family for their help. My special thanks go to Mrs. Isobel Brock, the daughter of R.S. Williams Jr., for photographs, other family documents, and reminiscences, but in particular for her time and great understanding.

I am very thankful for the help of these institutions and individuals: City of Toronto Archives; Metropolitan Toronto Central Library; the Ontario Archives in Toronto; the Public Archives in Ottawa; the National Library, Music Division, in Ottawa; the Library of the Music Faculty of the University of Toronto; the Library of the Ontario Institute for Studies in Education in Toronto; the Corporation of Hamilton Public Library in Hamilton, Ontario; London Public Libraries in London, Ontario; D. Stuart Kennedy of Calgary, Alberta; T. Seamen and David Jafelice, organists of St. Paul's Roman Catholic Church in Toronto; Gabriel M. Kney of London, Ontario; Dieter M. Geissler of Keates Organ Co. Ltd. in Acton, Ontario; Dubay Organ Ltd. in Burlington, Ontario; Rev. R.G. Gardner of Cayuga, Ontario; Father Steven Somerville in Midland, Ontario; Bob Witham, organist of St. Margaret's Roman Catholic Church in Midland, Ontario; Gordon L. Angus of Willowdale, Ontario; Mrs. Jo Aldwinckle of Oshawa, Ontario; Remenyi House of Music and Michael Remenyi in Toronto, Ontario.

I am very grateful to Thomas Bouckley of Oshawa for photographs from his rare collection.

I must express my sincere appreciation to Dr. Helmut Kallmann for encouragement and support during my research. I am greatly indebted to Professor C. Morey, Dr. Frederick A. Hall, Dr. John W. Hayes, and Mrs. Sharon Hick for much useful criticism and help.

Many thanks to Brian Boyle, studio photographer of the Royal Ontario Museum, for producing the photographic documentation used in this book.

I am grateful to all whose contributions are acknowledged in the text and with the illustrations.

PREFACE

Musical-instrument manufacturing was one of the few areas in which Canada was able to compete with the United States and England in the nineteenth and early twentieth centuries. This book describes one of the leading firms in the music industry in Canada at that time. The Toronto business that was conducted under the sign of the "Big Fiddle" added significantly to the spread of music in the city and province. The founder of this family business was Richard Sugden Williams; with his son, R.S. Williams Jr., he is also responsible for amassing what is perhaps the earliest collection of musical instruments in Canada, and what is certainly one of the largest.

The unexpected scarcity of sources prolonged my research to almost a decade. The Williamses' business ended abruptly, leaving barely the documents necessary to reconstruct the family's business and private life. A few family documents and reminiscences have helped to bridge this gap. In many instances, however, even the available sources had to be rejected because of inaccuracy. Despite such difficulties, reflected particularly in the presentation of the Williamses' private life, this book ventures to disclose the growth of the Williams' enterprise, its advances in technology and commerce, and the social context in which the business grew.

Of great documentary significance and value to this book were the catalogues published by the R.S. Williams' firm that I consulted during my research. Of the ten catalogues cited in this book, three can be found as part of the R.S. Williams Collection in the Royal Ontario Museum. The rest reside in the National Library of Canada in Ottawa and in the personal collection of Michael Remenyi in Toronto.

The R.S. Williams Collection of European and other musical instruments is now in the European Department of the Royal Ontario Museum. The description of the collection's growth, and some details of the instruments themselves, are included to allow both the historian and the general reader to assess the significance of the collection.

In the hope that my research on the Williams family will be useful to all readers, I share most of my findings about the family in this book; I believe that there can never be too much information bringing to life people of the past, people who have made our history.

RICHARD SUGDEN WILLIAMS: THE EARLY YEARS (1834-1856)

Immigration and settlement of the Williams family in Ontario; R.S. Williams' school years; the path to an unexpected profession.

The early nineteenth century saw the beginning of musical-instrument manufacture in Canada. A barrel-operated organ made by Richard Coates in 1820 can still be seen in the Church of the Children of Peace at Sharon, Ontario. Pierre Olivier Lyonais was active as early as 1825 as Canada's first known professional violin maker. Piano building started in the province of Quebec, with makers such as Frederick Hund (c. 1816), G.W. Mead (c. 1827), and J.M. Thomas (c. 1832).[1] Although Richard Sugden Williams was not among these earliest instrument makers, he nonetheless was one of the important followers who built on the foundation laid by the first Canadian craftsmen. He helped establish the industry and raise public interest in music. Indeed, an important part of understanding the development of this industry in Canada is appreciating Williams' role in it.

On April 12, 1834, a son was born to Richard and Jane Williams of Great George Street in London, England. He was christened Richard Sugden Williams at St. Margaret's Church beside Westminster Abbey on August 3, 1834, and was raised in London for four years. The boy's life was then suddenly changed by his parent's decision to emigrate to Canada. The reasons for this decision have never been recorded; it is impossible to know whether the Williamses left to escape the stormy events of troubled Britain in the 1830s, or whether they were motivated by personal and family considerations.

The long ocean voyage to Halifax was followed by what was at that time an equally arduous trip by bateau, steamer, stage coach, and again by steamer to Toronto. It is possible that news of the Rebellion in Toronto reached the Williamses as they neared the end of their journey. For this or other reasons, the family decided against staying in the capital of the province and went instead to Hamilton. Richard Williams is described in the local records of that city as a retired gentleman.[2] A second son, William Hodgson Williams, was born in Hamilton in 1839. In 1841, when both children were still quite young, the family moved to Toronto. These two Canadian cities, Hamilton and Toronto, were to provide R.S. Williams with the beginnings of a career in musical instruments.

Thanks to his parents, Richard Sugden Williams belonged to the one-third of children who benefited from the education system. (The rest did not attend school at all.) His education started in a Toronto common school organized according to the First General Common School Act of Canada of 1840. The majority of his schoolmates were boys and girls from ordinary families of workers, farmers, and small tradespeople. "The boy received a common school education, chiefly under the tuition of the late Mr. Darby, a master of the olden time, not easily forgotten by the school boys of that day."[3] The pioneer schools provided a strict and formal education: R.S. Williams would have been encouraged to be obedient and respectful to his elders and to be uncritical in the acceptance of concepts and notions approved by the authorities. Independence of thought was discouraged.[4] One wonders what factors in his personal and family life enabled Williams to overcome these restrictive elements in his early training and to put his education to good use in his rise to business and social success.

Having in mind R.S. Williams' later career, one looks to his boyhood for influences on his personal attitude towards the world of music. There is good reason to believe that the stream of such influence did not flow from the years of his school education. In the elementary schools of that time musical instrument was absent, and even singing was dependent on the good nature, enthusiasm, and ability of the teacher.

In searching for the origin of the Williamses' tradition as musical-instrument makers, one reporter who interviewed R.S. Williams suggested that, as his forefathers for several generations had been builders, the famous Canadian piano manufacturer inherited the building instinct naturally.[5] The persuasive-

Record of R.S. Williams' baptism. (Courtesy Dean and Chaper of Westminster.)

ness of this idea fades, however, when no documentary evidence is found. R.S. Williams' father was a cook; none of the grandchildren of the founder of the family music business recalls any predecessor following a career in musical-instrument manufacturing.

The assumption that R.S. Williams inherited his interest in musical instruments might be based on a misinterpretation of a story about a family heirloom, a violoncello that was made by Jane Williams' grandfather and which the Williamses brought to Canada. The shape and workmanship of this instrument, included in the R.S. Williams Collection now in the Royal Ontario Museum, reveal a rather naïve imitation. It might be supposed, however, that the old cello, as the most peculiar piece of the family furnishings, might have drawn the boy's attention. R.S. Williams' ultimate career suggests that his early curiosity might have been aroused not by the playing, not by the sound itself, but by the cause of the sound, by the functioning of the instrument.

Strong hints of the boy's remarkable skill in the use of various tools appear in his biography, which also mentions his success in repairing various small musical instruments.[6] Perhaps young Williams was also influenced in his choice of career by the location near his school (and not far from his home) of a musical-instrument manufacturer's store and workshop, at 153 Elizabeth Street.[7] The manufacturer's name was William Townsend; Williams was apprenticed to him in 1846 to learn the piano, organ, and melodeon industries.[8] About Townsend himself, it is known that he came from New Hampshire, "the birthplace of the melodeon."[9] Jeremiah Carhart and others from Concord, New Hampshire, had introduced to Toronto the modern instrument with its suction bellows.[10] The article describes "Townsend & Co." as one of the leading melodeon manufacturing firms of Toronto in the 1840s. It seems, however, that all of this information originates with R.S. Williams. Except for the appearance of Townsend's name and occupation in city directories – musical-instrument manufacturer (Toronto), and organ builder (Hamilton) – little documentary evidence can be found about him and his business. Alas, not one of Townsend's instruments even appears in *Michel's Organ Atlas*, the popular and most comprehensive (for North America) source of such documentation.

Whatever the capabilities of William Townsend, his influence on the young R.S. Williams appears to have been remarkable, and the boy's parents made a good decision in apprenticing their son to him. The Statute of Artificers had been repealed in 1814 and after that time apprenticeship was on a voluntary basis; nevertheless, the custom of paying the master a sum of money as a consideration for accepting an apprentice remained.[11] Perhaps Richard Sugden's father paid Townsend the usual £10; perhaps the master did not take any money but accepted the boy as a favour to the parents and as a way of gaining a hand for his workshop and business for the traditional seven years.

At the time of Richard Sugden's apprenticeship, every part of the instrument had to be manufactured by hand. This gave the young craftsman excellent training and thorough proficiency in all details of the business. But the way to knowledge and skill was not simple. For example, a number of different operations were required to build a melodeon; the making of the case, bellows, and reed frame were the most essential.[12]

As would any other apprentice in the business, R.S. Williams must have been trained to make straight, clear pieces out of warped, checked, or knotty timber. Walnut and rosewood logs for resawing veneer were stored in the workshop along with sheets already prepared for use. The big vise saw would eventually have become familiar to the boy, who had to know how to resaw the logs held vertically in the vise. He would also have become familiar with the huge and heavy workbenches with holes on the top and in the legs for the holdfasts and the bench dog. Gradually he would have learned to use the jointing plane, the jack plane, the large smooth plane, and the small rabbet plane, the tools of the true cabinetmaker.

There was also the mechanical work: helping to cut pieces from sheets of brass for hinges; assisting in cutting frames for the reeds (or "brass" as they were generally called), narrow strips or tongues of thin, hard, yet elastic metal. As soon as the metal frames were ready, furnished with a rectangular aperture, these tongues were fastened above them by one end. This was entirely the masters' business, as was the voicing and regulating of the reeds.

A successful apprentice in musical-instrument building needed a number of skills and talents. He would have had to deal with a wide variety of problems, from repairing a cracked violin, to replacing the broken hammer of a pianoforte, to restoring the watchkey screw-mechanism of a one-hundred-year-old English guitar. Townsend must also have initiated Williams into the secrets of free-reed voicing and of the regulating and tuning of melodeons. This job was fairly complex, but the tools required were few: small half-round and flat files with a safe edge, a half-round steel burnisher, a pair of small round-nosed pliers, a watchmaker's hammer, a small scraper, a reed hook for taking the reeds from the panel, an ebony block, a block of polished steel for use as an anvil, and a steel slip for tuning.

There were other sorts of things that Townsend would have taught his talented apprentice. The young Williams must gradually have become familiar with the organization of the business. He would have learned the importance of gaining the trust of his co-workers and his customers alike.

In 1853 the seven-year apprenticeship ended; Richard Sugden Williams was a highly skilled journeyman. In the same year he moved to Hamilton with his master and their musical-instrument business.[13] The years in Hamilton marked a turning point in Williams' career and in his personal life. At nineteen years of age, he was introduced to a girl who had come to Hamilton with her parents from the United States just a year before Richard Sugden followed Townsend there. Her name was Sarah DeMain Norris; the daughter of Robert and Mary DeMain Norris. February 1854 saw the wedding of Richard Sugden Williams and Sarah. Their first child, Robert, was born November 29, 1854.

At this time the entire musical-instrument industry was shaken by a shrinking market, and a business such as Townsend's was vulnerable to such change. In 1855, just two years after the move to Hamilton, Townsend's company failed. The *London Free Press*, which got the story from R.S. Williams some forty years later, put it this way:"

> The change of location proved an unfortunate one financially, and they were forced to make an assignment. Mr. Williams...was induced to take hold of the bankrupt business, and he was not long in putting into it the hustling energy and forethought that has marked his career."[14]

All this happened when R.S. Williams had just entered his twenties, and only a rare dedication to his profession could have given him the enthusiasm and strength for the task of heading the whole business and managing it. He did manage it so well, in fact, that it would become the basis of his later success.

The entire year of 1855 kept Williams so busy with preparations for moving back to Toronto, a city of continuing rapid progress and of many positive signs that the roots of his business would be planted in fertile soil. Williams' frequent trips to Toronto must have made him aware that competition with businesses already flourishing there would be keen; however, visits to the music and musical-instrument dealers in Toronto would also have provided him with a number of possible business contacts. As it happened, all of these businesses were located on King Street: Joseph Harkness; Haycraft, Small & Addison; A. & S. Nordheimer; and John Thomas & Son.[15]

The Nordheimer brothers, Abraham and Samuel, had moved their business from Kingston to Toronto while Williams was working with Townsend in Hamilton. Theirs was the most prosperous firm of all, importing sheet music and pianos.

R.S. Williams must have been glad that the Nordheimers were not especially interested in melodeons. He originally planned to base his business on the manufacture of melodeons partly because of their popularity, partly because of his experience and skill in building them. However, early in 1855 came news that musical instruments, especially those imported for the use of military bands, were to be admitted into Canada free of duty. This may have influenced Williams to consider expanding his plans to include trading in imported instruments of this type. He must have become convinced that Toronto, then twice as big as Hamilton, would offer him a good business opportunity.

The move to Toronto was made. In the Directory of 1856, both Richard and R.S. Williams are listed, the former as "cook and confectioner," and the son as "melodeon manufacturer" and under "Music and Music Instrument Dealers" in the "Professional and trades directory" section.[16] Although Hamilton remained important as a turning point in R.S. Williams' life and in the life of his family, Toronto was the city in which the family business was to flourish for decades to come.

2

STARTING OUT UNDER THE BIG FIDDLE (1856-1864)

Toronto's musical climate; establishment of the new firm; early achievements.

When Richard Sugden Williams accomplished his goal of returning to Toronto and establishing his own business, the city was in the midst of rapid growth and varied development. Many of its citizens showed a lively interest in music; churches, cultural institutions and associations flourished, providing many opportunities for the young musical-instrument builder and dealer.

In 1856 the population of Toronto was 41,760, and the desire of this large community to be actively involved in and entertained by good music was served by the Toronto Philharmonic Society, which had offices and rooms in the St. Lawrence Hall. In these premises performances of the Toronto Vocal Musical Society and the Metropolitan Choral Society also took place, and world-renowned artists such as the soprano Jenny Lind performed there.[17]

But there were many other centres catering to Torontonians' love of music. As shown by the historical buildings that have been preserved, money went into many civic improvements; some of the best buildings for music, notably the St. Lawrence Hall, were built between 1849, the year of the great fire, and 1856, which marked the return of Richard Sugden Williams to Toronto. The buildings of the Normal and Model Schools were opened in 1851, and Trinity College was completed in 1856. These schools significantly helped the growing interest in music, not only by teaching but also by their involvement in performance, which served to educate the public musically.

One expression of the growing interest in music was the cultivation of music in the home. Indeed, it became a custom among well-to-do families in the city to own either a piano or a less expensive melodeon. These instruments, however, were used less for serious music than for amusement, the owners being satisfied with the ability to play light, entertaining melodies, decidedly an asset in a young lady of marriageable age.

On the other hand, more serious instrumentalists could be inspired by the array of musical life brought to the city by the military bands, and the travelling companies, the visiting actors. Except for a few music teachers, these instrumentalists were almost all amateurs and members of the local brass bands (which in Toronto-York existed as early as 1824), of the Toronto Philharmonic Society, or of other vocal and instrumental groups.

Thus the demand for musical instruments of almost all types was growing rapidly. The number of professional musicians, and of teachers and professors of music in Toronto in 1856 was seventeen, according to the professional and trades directory.

That same year 1856 saw added to Toronto's musical-instrument makers and importers a new firm under the sign of the "Big Fiddle." About eighty years later Richard Sugden Williams Jr., the son of the founder, remarked,

> "My father selected as a trade mark the sign of the Big Fiddle, which he had made of tin. It was larger than a double bass and was hung over his old store in the Le Pages Block on Yonge Street."[18]

According to the sequence of documented events, before being moved to mark the workshop at 206 Yonge Street, the sign must have identified the Williams workshop at 144 Yonge Street (the Le Pages Block) for four years.

The local records reflect the development of R.S. Williams' musical-instrument firm and give an indication of its expanding range of services. R.S. Williams is introduced in 1856 as "melodeon manufacturer."[19] The assessment roll for the Ward of St. James in the City of Toronto, 1857, includes R.S. Williams, organ builder by profession, residing in a house owned by a Mr. George Maver; for the next two years Williams is listed as "music dealer."[20] In the Directory of 1859-60, R.S. Williams is listed as a "dealer in music and musical instruments, pianoforte tuner, & c., 206 Yonge St." and also under "Music Sellers, & c."[21] The new address at 143 Yonge Street appears in 1861, at which time R.S. Williams is listed under the heading "Piano Makers and Turners" (the last word being a mistake for "Tuners"), but here his profession is designated as "dealer."[22]

Unfortunately this significant period in the growth of the Williams business was suddenly overshadowed by the death of R.S. Williams' father, although there exist some discrepancies about the exact date. Richard Williams, father of Richard Sudgen Williams, lived as a retired gentleman in Hamilton till 1854. "He then moved to Toronto, and soon became contracted with the Northern Railway, at the opening of which he was accidentally killed at Newmarket." The name and occupation of the person killed are identical to those of the young businessman's father.[23] This brings into question the information cited above that lists Richard Williams on Sayer Street in 1856.[24] There is no hint of the

Sarah Williams, b. DeMain Norris, in 1878.
Courtesy Mrs. I.W. Brock, b. Williams, Toronto.

fate of Williams' mother, Jane; the only record of her is on his birth certificate. Richard Sugden's younger brother, William Hodgson, helped him in the workshop in the early years of the business, but later struck out on his own, moving to Baltimore, Maryland, where he spent the rest of his life.[25]

Nevertheless, strong family ties appear to have been important to the young R.S. Williams, and the growth of his musical-instrument enterprise coincided with the growth of his own family. Robert Williams, the son of Richard Sugden and Sarah, became a pupil at the Model School in Toronto. Sarah gave birth to a daughter, Anne (later known also as Anna and as Annie), in June of 1857. A second son, Frank, was born in September 1859, but died two years later, just when another daughter, Henrietta, was born.

Conditions were favourable for the musical-instrument trade in Toronto, and R.S. Williams took advantage of this in the early days of his business to produce a wide variety of instruments. From the list of diplomas and prizes that he received it is clear that Williams' early efforts were well received in the city and in the province.[26] The originals of these awards are in the Royal Ontario Museum, and the diplomas are of remarkable documentary value.

The collection of prize tags includes twenty-one first or extra prize tags: six lack the name of the organizer and the date of the exhibition; one, updated, is from the Agricultural Association of Upper Canada; and fourteen show the title, place, and dates of exhibitions between 1864 and 1888. The variety of instruments for which these prize tags were awarded reveals the variety of R.S. Williams' activity as a musical-instrument manufacturer. There is an extra prize tag from the Union Exhibition in Toronto in 1864 for the "Victoria Organ and Harmonium" and a second from the same exhibition for a "Collection of Drums and Drum Heads." From the Provincial and Agricultural Exhibition in 1865 there is a first prize for a "Double-Banked 12-Stop Organ." The Agricultural and Arts Association Exhibition in 1870 brought a "1st Extra Prize" for "Melodeon & Organ Reeds & Keys," and for a "Cabinet or Parlour Organ." The Peterborough Central Exhibition in 1888 made an award to the firm of R.S. Williams & Son for "Pianos"; but this tag belongs to the later years of Williams' achievements.

An even clearer picture of the young musical-instrument maker's activities is given by two illustrated cata-

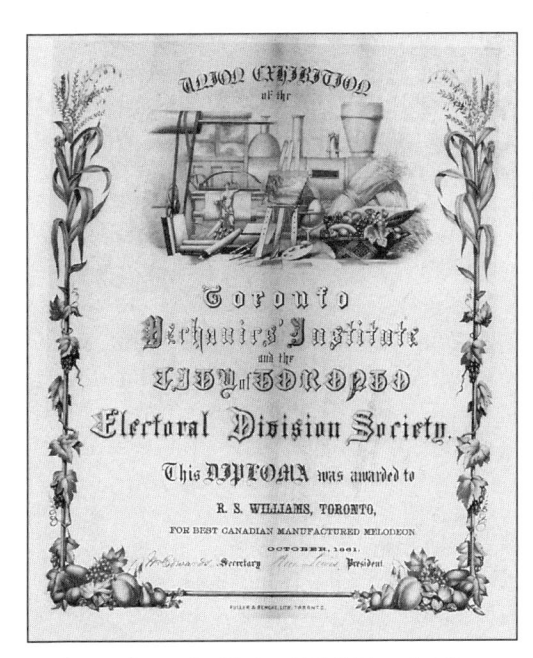

Diploma from the Union Exhibition for the best Canadian manufactured melodeon, 1861.

logues produced for his firm in these early years; one was published in 1862, the other in 1864. Like the diplomas and prize tags, they inform us that Williams' main interest remained the building of melodeons and reed organs, the skills he had mastered at the beginning of his professional career. For the first time is given something of R.S. Williams' philosophy of melodeon manufacture:

> "The success attending the first Catalogue that I issued some two years ago, leads to the necessity of another issue, in which I shall endeavor to show to the public of Canada, particularly those of Upper Canada, that I am now manufacturing Melodeons not only equal, but superior to any made in the United States. It is a well-known fact that there is not a Melodeon maker in the States but what he has some little improvement of his own, for which he procures a patent, thus debarring each other in a great measure in arriving at perfection. It is not unreasonable in supposing that if all the improvements on Melodeons that have been patented in the States were combined, that we should then have from them a much better instrument than we now have; and it is in this particular that I claim for my instruments a superiority over those made in the States. I combine all the improvements up to the present time. I voice and tune every instrument myself, at which I have had twelve years' practical experience. I have also practical workmen that have had many years' experience in the States. In fact I have now every facility for manufacturing a superior instrument to any yet offered to the public."[27]

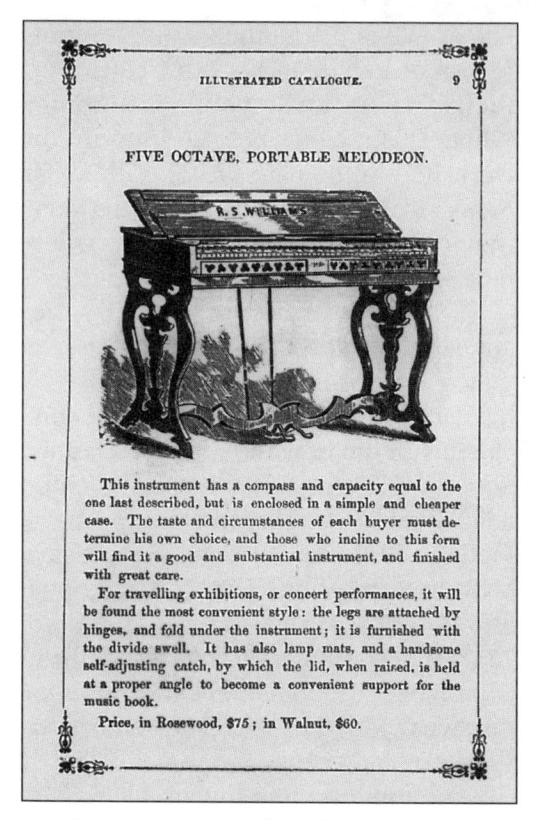

The five octave, portable melodeon on page 9 of the catalogue, 1862.

Mention of a previous catalogue that had bee issued two years earlier indicates remarkable speed in achieving the recognition of the public and of representative institutions of business and commerce.

The variety of melodeons offered, illustrated in the 1862 catalogue with woodcut reproductions, is surprisingly rich. R.S. Williams offers piano-style single- or double-reed melodeons of six or five octave compass, and four-and-a-half or five octave portable melodeons of classical style. The illustrations of many of these instruments which appear in the catalogue are much better than any descriptive information. The prices of the melodeons advertised in this catalogue range from $40 to $150. Certainly these prices were not within the reach of a labourer whose average wage was below a dollar per day. Who were Williams' customers? The question is partially answered in the list of testimonials in the catalogue, which represents another significant documentary source and serves as a clue to R.S. Williams' success. On pages 12-19 of the 1862 catalogue there are twenty-five opinions and statements from institutional and individual customers or from professionals who tested the melodeons. These pages disclose some important evaluations of the quality and popularity of the Williams melodeons.

Of course, as with all such testimonials and opinions used as advertising, the content is very favourable. Some of the statements, however, are very specific. J. McCarroll, who visited the Williams manufactory, compliments the melodeons on being "at once ornamental and melodious," especially suited to those "in favour of home manufacturers."[28]

Testimonials from music instructors seem to emphasize the quality of Williams melodeons as compared to others. W. Labitzky, identified as a "Professor of Music," finds the melodeons to be "very superior Instruments in tone as well as workmanship."[29] H.F. Sefton, Music Master of the Normal, Model, and Grammar Schools of Toronto, was very specific about the advantages of the Williams instrument:

"...and above all, by the method of voicing adopted, the very objectionable *hurdy-girdy-like* scream which too frequently attends instruments of this class is entirely overcome, and rendered perfect."[30]

An attentive reader is well able to imagine the good and bad points of the Williams melodeons as compared with those of other makers.

In addition to testimonials by customers and music professionals, the catalogue quotes those involved in the sale of the instruments. Mr. Allin of Oshawa, an agent for Williams melodeons, was asked by R.S. Williams if his melodeons satisfied the purchasers, and answered as follows:

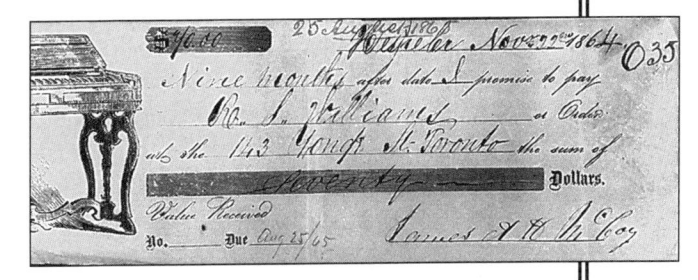

Cheque of the R.S. Williams' firm, November 22nd, 1864. Courtesy Mrs. I.W. Brock, b. Williams, Toronto.

"I must say that, of the large number I have sold, I have not heard of a single complaint... and my opinion of your instrument is, that they are better tone than any imported one that I have seen, and in the action and working part, they are far superior to Prince & Smith's [Buffalo, N.Y.]." Mr. Allin is then quoted as asking for more "4 octave Walnut Melodeons," because he has sold the last half-dozen sent him.[31]

Concerning the price, of interest is a letter from the Reverend Richard H. Harris of Brock, dated April 9, 1862 and reprinted in the catalogue:

"With respect to the Piano Melodeon which I purchased from your for one of the churches in my parish, I think it but right to say that its excellence and sweetness of tone were very generally admired. I would recommend your Melodeons, at $90, for use in country churches."[32]

The range of melodeon prices obviously accommodated the purchase of instruments for use in homes, churches, and places of musical instruction.

The variety of musical instruments and accessories offered tells us something about R.S. Williams' attitude to the musical-instrument trade: he valued variety, and felt it important to offer a wide range of merchandise and service. In the 1862 catalogue he offers violins, violoncello and double-bass strings, as well as string sets for guitars. Williams also carried flutes and fifes, favourites with many music-loving immigrants from Britain or other European countries who had brought them to their new homeland.[33] A price list of drums shows a variety of these instruments in stock. An advertisement gives further information about Williams' other important activities: the firm offered tuning and repair of pianos, melodeons, flutinas, concertinas, and accordions, and the trade of secondhand pianos and melodeons.

The buying and trading of secondhand instruments can be considered one of the most important sources of the R.S. Williams' collection of musical instruments. According to an inventory of diplomas and prizes, published about eighty years later, Richard Sugden Williams was awarded a "Diplomas of Toronto Mechanics Institute, City of Toronto, for collection of musical instruments," dated 1861; it is now in the possession of Robert Williams, great-grandson of R.S. Williams, in Toronto. It not only indicates Williams' role in the early period of musical-instrument collecting, but is also one of the earliest proofs of this sort of activity in Canada. There is good reason to believe that R.S. Williams started to collect old and rare musical instruments at the beginning of his successful business in Toronto. Undoubtedly the first specimen in his collection was the unsophisticated violoncello made by his mother's grandfather in the Isle of Wight.

Although there are few documents about his practice as a collector, Williams did have a great opportunity to acquire, through exchange or trade, fine examples of old guitars, violins, flutes, clarinets, and other instruments.

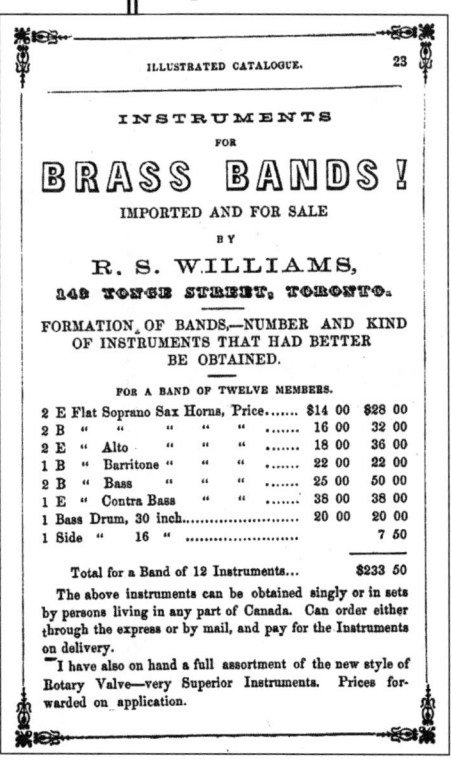

Instruments of brass bands on page 23 of the catalogue, 1862.

His collection was later enriched by his son, Richard Sugden Williams Jr., but it is clear that R.S. Williams amassed the foundation of the collection from early in his career. In addition to string and reed instruments, brass band instruments were also offered for sale; trade in these instruments would have provided further opportunities for Williams to add to his collection

The last page of the catalogue offers "Bound books of instructions for different instruments." The list includes *Cook's Vocal singing* (sic) as well as Lablanche's work on the same subject.[34] The books of instruction for violin are represented by the works of Louis Spohr (1784-1859), a great German violinist and composer, and of Jacques-Féréol Mazas (1782-1849), French violinist and composer. For the violoncello there is the work of the famous German violoncellist Bernhard Romberg (1767-1811), *Method for the violoncellos*, originally published in Berlin by Trautenwein in 1840. The catalogue also offers books of instruction for accordion and concertina, indicating the remarkable growth in popularity of these two types of portable free-reed keyboard instruments, dating back to the year 1822 when the accordion was invented.

The sign of the Big Fiddle seems to have been a good omen for the fledgling Williams' enterprise. As shown by the numerous prizes and diplomas, and by the quality and variety of the instruments offered in his first catalogues, Richard Sugden Williams attained an impressive measure of success in even the few years following the establishment of his musical instrument business in Toronto.

3

R.S. WILLIAMS AND THE FREE-REED ORGAN (1864-1870)

The Victoria Organ; the struggle for new goals.

Through the 1860s, business under the sign of the Big Fiddle was succeeding, and the young R.S. Williams was becoming known particularly as a significant pioneer in the introduction and development of the free-reed organ in Canada. His continuing interest in building and improving these instruments is evident in the catalogue of 1864, assumed to be the third issued by his firm. Williams' purpose in building and trading in melodeons was, at least in part, to contribute to the popularization of music in Canada:

"The universal attention now paid to the cultivation of music throughout Canada is one of the most encouraging features in our civilization. Not only in cities and in large social centers, but in remote villages and farming communities, a taste for music and a more or less facility in its performance may be found. No instruments in modern times have done more to carry this blessing into families, and to furnish choirs with a valuable accompaniment than the MELODEON."[35]

The 1864 catalogue also reveals the growth of the family of free-reed keyboard instruments in Canada; it introduces a new type of instrument, larger than the Williams melodeon, called the "Victoria Organ." The general description of this instrument informs the potential customer of some remarkable changes to the harmonium in its musical and aesthetic qualities:

"An improvement on the Harmonium, which it resembles in external appearance – and acknowledged by competent judges to be the best instrument of the kind ever made – powerful in tone, rich organ-like in quality, even and prompt in touch, allowing the performer to execute the most rapid music. A double bellows of peculiar construction, is employed in the VICTORIA ORGAN. It is more easily operated and more completely under the control of the performer than other descriptions of bellows, having two blow pedals so placed that they are operated by the feet with the greatest facility. By its means the instrument is supplied with several times as powerful a current of wind as can be produced by the Melodeon bellows. When it is remembered that, other things being equal, the volume of tone must depend on the amount of wind supplied, it will be seen that this improvement is of the first importance."[36]

A more specific description of the two-manual Victoria Organ confirms the improvements over the usual two types of melodeon in production at the time:

"2 Banks Keys, 12 Stops, 5 Set Reeds, Tremolo, Sub Bass, Basso Tenuto Swell, & C. ... Simple in construction, no at all liable to get out of order. The Sub Bass is a new improvement in these instruments corresponding to the pedal in a large organ, and is attached to the keys, doing away with the foot pedals: foot pedals can be added to these instruments if desired. The Tremolo, as the name denotes, causes a tremulous tone with which fine effects can be produced. The Basso Tenuto stop holds one or more keys down till the next is pressed down, thus leaving the left hand free to activate the other bank of keys."[37]

Also offered are a four-stop Victoria Organ of five octave compass, designed for small-country churches, and two other instruments of the same type. The description of the new Victoria Organ, along with the price, reveals that it is intended as a less expensive alternative to larger organs. The catalogue emphasizes that its musical features make it "equal to an organ costing $800 to $1000."[38] In comparison, the double-banked Victoria Organ cost $300 in walnut and $350 in rosewood.[39] And to make such an instrument affordable to a wider variety of people, Williams also offered an even less expensive alternative: "The same instrument, with only one bank of keys, 10 stops, I make in walnut, for $250, and Rosewood $300."[40]

Victoria Organ on page 7 of the catalogue, 1864.

The catalogue goes on to cite the response to the introduction of the Victoria Organ. These notes were inspired by R.S. Williams' participation in the Provincial Exhibition at Kingston in September 1863, where the diploma "for an Organ Harmonium" was awarded to the young instrument builder. A rather flattering passage from Toronto *The Globe* (Toronto) tells what kind of instrument the Victoria Organ was and says that its production was begun in 1863.

"Musical instruments: R.S. Williams, of Toronto, made a very fine display of Harmonium and Melodeons in the late show; one in particular, an organ Harmonium

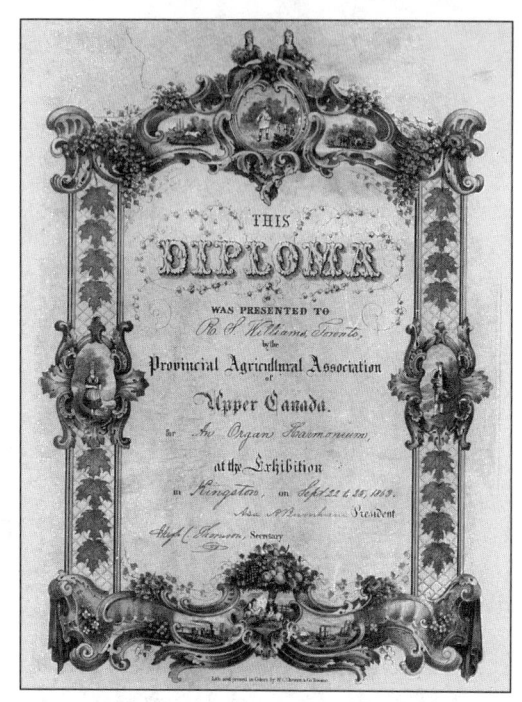

Diploma by the Provincial Agricultural Association of Upper Canada for an organ harmonium, 1863.

(named, we understand by the workmen, the "Victoria Organ") which for its beauty and variety of harmony, can hardly be excelled in America. Upon this instrument the performer can produce the softest strains with a tremulous effort if desired or (by means of the appropriate stops) the stronger and more dignified church melodies, with all the intermediate varieties of organ or melodeon music."

The article goes on to describe the bellows mechanism, so improved

"that a child of ten years can play its utmost power with ease. ... and altogether it is an instrument of rare excellence and reflects great credit upon the manufacturer, as well as the workmen, of whom the best are employed."

The writer describes and commends the other instruments displayed by Williams at the exhibition, and concludes that "Mr. Williams...may justly feel proud of the success that attends his efforts."[41]

The different names by which the new instrument was known give use some indication of its position in the family of free-reed keyboard instruments. Contemporary journals introduce the instrument as the "Organ Harmonium, or the Victoria Organ,"[42] describing it as "a new class of instrument manufactured by R.S.W., Toronto."[43] In another article, instead of reference to the "Victoria Organ," is mentioned an instrument described as a "Harmonium with two banks of keys."[44] The article in *The Globe* is the clearest description of R.S. Williams' new instrument, and it mentions both harmoniums and melodeons, the former being identified as Victoria Organs. R.S. Williams himself considered the instrument a harmonium to which he added newly developed improvements.[45]

These much lauded improvements and "new" developments did not, however, originate with R.S. Williams. His Victoria Organ was, in fact, basically identical to the organ harmonium and the cabinet organ begin produced in the United States, where there were many more advanced and experienced builders of these instruments. Williams openly admitted the influence of American improvements.[46] He was perhaps most affected by the harmonium with suction wind constructed by Estey of Brattleboro, Vermont, and by Mason &

Hamlin in Boston. The first Mason & Hamlin Organ Harmonium was made and sold in 1855, and it was patented in 1856. In 1861 the firm changed the name of their reed organ to "Cabinet Organ." The introduction and production of the harmonium-type reed organ offered the public an instrument with considerably more musical capability than the earlier melodeons. R.S. Williams, with the same objective, began the production of his Victoria Organ in Canada nearly a decade later.

There was little room in this work for a lengthy explanation of the characteristics of the rich family of free-reed keyboard instruments. It should be noted, however, that the harmonium was first patented in Paris by Alexandre Debain in 1840. In it, the tones are produced by the vibration of free reeds under the pressure of air. The equivalent of a harmonium – the term used in Europe – is the American organ, working on wind drawn inward through the reeds by means of suction bellows. Thus, what was produced by Estey and by Mason & Hamlin in America, and by R.S. Williams eight years later in Canada, was the American organ, going by the names organ harmonium, cabinet organ, and Victoria Organ. These instruments have prominent external features: the keyboard and the treadles. The case, unlike that of the portable or the piano-style melodeon, houses the entire apparatus for supplying the wind to the pan and to the whole playing structure; therefore, it was designed as a low-backed cabinet with a flat top consisting of a cover and a folding music desk.

R.S. Williams' two-manual Victoria Organ did, however, reveal some advance over the American organ when it was first produced in Canada. The Victoria Organ was supplied with a powerful current of wind from enlarged bellows which, with the two exhausters, were placed vertically below the pan. Operating one and then the other blow pedal allowed the exhausters to open and close alternately, ensuring that a steady current of air was drawn inward by the empty bellows through the vibrating metal reeds. Certainly such an improvement made possible the production of instruments of higher musical quality. Compared with organs made up to this time, the curvature of the reeds was more pronounced and the voicing stronger in this first Victoria Organ. The two-manual organ with five sets of reeds, a sub bass giving thirteen extra bass notes of sixteen foot pitch, a tremolo, and a basso tenuto would have been unthinkable without the assurance of a steady and strong suction. The twelve draw stops were placed beyond the ends of the keyboard, as in a pipe organ. The swell shutters were operated by foot levers beside the treadles.

Compared with the trestle, portable, and piano-style melodeons, the Victoria Organ was a new and aesthetically very different kind of instrument. The upright case was actually just an empty box open at the bottom, was adaptable to changing tastes and contemporary styles, and allowed rapid changes in carving and other sorts of embellishment. In the late 1870s, it appeared as a large, complicated piece of furniture with a purely decorative top, which sometimes extended the height of the case to seven feet. Because of its grandeur the organ was usually displayed in the best room in the house, the salon or parlour, to add to the prestige of the family. Thus was secured for the later cabinet organ the well-known term "parlour organ."

Developments in the design as well as in the musical capabilities of the instruments were influenced by the American builders. This is evident from similarities among instruments produced by various firms. R.S. Williams was inspired by the flourishing American production of instruments, particularly in the blossoming free-reed organ industry. It can be assumed that he, like other Canadian producers, must have used pattern books such as *The Cabinet Maker's Assistant* by John Hall (the first American pattern book, published in 1840), as well as treatises, catalogues, articles, or other works on furniture design. He would also have considered the cases of existing keyboard instruments when designing his own. For example, the trestle of one of Williams' melodeons has bandsawn shapes and a veneered surface, which might have been inspired by Hall's *Assistant*. A melodeon of 1857 by Mason & Hamlin has an almost identical trestle, though their first model, made in 1854, had one of a different shape. Comparison of the Mason & Hamlin melodeon with instruments by R.S. Williams in 1860 and by Carhart and Needham in 1866 provoke the question of whether Williams and the two leading American firms reached the uniform shape of the melodeon trestles as a result of using the same design source, or whether one copied it from another. Legs, music racks, pedal lyres, and other parts of the instrument were designed in contemporary style to satisfy the fashion-conscious public.[47] The public was acquainted with modern and fashionable instruments through catalogues, advertisements, and music journals; they also saw them in the stores, and this stimulated the import of even more American instruments.

The Toronto City Directories for the years surrounding R.S. Williams' introduction of the Victoria Organ show a steady increase in the number of musical-instrument manufacturers and dealers. In the 1861 *Brown's Toronto General Directory*, for example, Richard B. Butland, who was registered in the previous year, advertises the sale of Carhart's and Prince's melodeons. This addition was part of the rise in listings of music dealers from four in 1859-1860 to eleven in 1861.[48] An 1864 advertisement appeared for the newly established Toronto, firm, T.F. Roome's Organ Manufactory, in operation during the years when the Victoria Organ was achieving wide acceptance. This was the same year that R.S. Williams was introduced in the listings as a manufacturer of melodeons and harmoniums, as well as an importer of music and musical instruments.[49] All of this information point to one very important factor in the readiness to adopt the new styles being produced by the American builders – competition.

Needless to say, the import activities must have kept all of the manufacturers on their toes. Only those most sensitive to novelty in the features and structure of the imported instruments were able to succeed, through a careful selection of instruments for sale or through hasty application of these stylistic or structural innovations to their own manufacture. Thus, after a relatively short delay, instruments produced in Canada differed very little from those made in the neighbouring states of America. As mentioned, details on the trestle melodeons made by R.S. Williams were comparable to those on the earlier or contemporary American instruments of the same type. Moreover, some close similarities can also be observed between the piano-style melodeons made by firms such as Smith Brothers of Boston, Waters of New York, and Pratt of Winchester, New Hampshire, and the same type made by R.S. Williams in the early 1860s. For example, the pierced trefoil ornaments on the lower grilles of these melodeons seem, at first glance, to be identical. A closer look, however, reveals a difference in the position of the motif, which in the Williams models is set aslant. This is a very slight difference, indeed, but one which is an original characteristic of the maker's work. (The practical purpose of piercing the grille is the same in all cases, to allow sound from the reeds.)

Judging by his achievements as an apprentice and journeyman with Townsend, and particularly from his success after founding his own workshop, it can be assumed that R.S. Williams had a sharp eye for form and for improvements to the instruments on show or in catalogues. His expertise in building instruments also helped him to know how to construct better and less expensive instruments with a few added touches to appeal to the public. His catalogues repeatedly affirm that differences in price depend on the cabinetmaker's work rather than on the musical capability of the instrument; hence the walnut-cased instrument is less expensive than the rosewood one, although "its mechanism, reeds, etc. are as perfect as in the costlier Melodeons."[50]

Williams' success, however, did not rest solely on his ability to perceive and adapt trends in style. The care he had taken for the musical qualities of his instruments since the beginning of his career is best shown by his involvement in the essential and creative work of voicing and tuning the reeds. In his earliest catalogues he stresses his own participation in this operation, of the greatest importance in the making of good instruments: "I voice and tune every instrument myself, at which I have had twelve years' practical experience."[51]

In the voicing of reeds, as in other aspects of the musical-instrument industry, the American influence was enormous. The first U.S. patent related to reed voicing was granted on June 19, 1849 to Charles C. Austin of Concord, New Hampshire. However, the well-known firm of G.A. Prince in Buffalo is presumed to be the prime and earliest source for improvements in voicing and regulating the reeds which were adopted by R.S. Williams' teacher, Townsend. A reprint of an 1873 article by Prince, published in the *Musical Courier* of April 22, 1875, credits Emmons Hamlin with advances in reed voicing. While employed as superintendent of tuning by George A. Prince and Co. of Buffalo, New York, Hamlin

> "did devise and invent a system we did adopt [at G.A. Prince], and have continued to use up to the present time. Furthermore, my long experience in the music business in the city of Boston and elsewhere previous to that date, justifies me in the belief that he is the original inventor of the said method of voicing reeds."[52]

This certification by the well-known producer of reed organs does not, however, change the fact that Hamlin never patented his discovery.

It can be assumed that melodeon makers in Canada, like Townsend, could not fail to notice the improved musical quality of instruments made across the border. It is not known if Townsend gained the information about voicing through consultation with George Prince or with Emmons Hamlin in Buffalo, or if he replicated the process through analyzing Prince's instruments imported to Toronto. However, Williams, as Townsend's successor, sheds more light on the matter. Williams' bold claim, to have incorporated in his new instruments all previous improvements, does seem to reflect the way in which innovations in the building of instruments were transmitted at the time.

For example, a list of early reed-organ patents in the United States gives us an idea of what was available to the Canadian melodeon maker, listing inventions patented between 1818 and 1856, up to the time that Williams started his own business. There were forty-one such patents, a considerable number of inventions in a relatively short time, but one which apparently left room for improvements such as those introduced by R.S. Williams. It should be mentioned that between 1824, when the Canadian Patent Office came into existence, and 1856, no Canadian patent on free-reed keyboard instruments was recorded.

The ability of Canadian producers to use existing American inventions served as an incentive for the Canadian makers of musical instruments to adopt these new ideas and techniques.

"It was not until 1869 that persons other than British subjects could obtain a Canadian patent, so there was nothing to prevent Canadian manufacturers from copying American devices, so long as they did not sell their products in the United States. Similarly, Canadian inventors could incorporate American patented ideas in their own claims."[53]

The transmission of new techniques was also abetted by the immigration to Canada of skilled and specialized workers with many years' experience in the United States. An article in the *Christian Guardian* remarks on this point; after writing about the Victoria Organ the reporter informs us that

"Mr. W. is still manufacturing melodeons of all styles and sizes. We had the pleasure of going through his manufactory, which is the largest in Canada. The work is carried on in different departments, under the charge of competent foremen. Most of the workmen have been procured from the large factories in the states."[54]

These notes confirm that in 1863 and early 1864 R.S. Williams' production was well-organized, being based on the work of various departments, each responsible for the manufacture of different parts; thus each instrument was the result of the specialized skills and experience of a number of workers. There is no reason to doubt that a similar organization of production was practiced in other firms at the time.

In an interview with R.S. Williams

much later in his life, the *London Free Press* reported that Williams was the only reed-organ producer in Canada;[55] this is false. In 1856, the year of the establishment of Williams' business, makers such as Andrus Brothers in London, and O'Neil, T.F. Roome, and Dalton of Toronto were also active. It is true, however, that R.S. Williams was the leading producer of reed organs in Canada in the first decade of his manufacturing activity. The same *London Free Press* interview describes, in R.S. Williams' own words, how he "took advantage of the opportunity to make a fortune."

"At the outbreak of the American War...money was very plentiful in the Northern States, and the American organ manufacturers were so crowded with home orders that they refused to book an order from a Canadian jobber unless the cash accompanied it, and then the date of delivery was not guaranteed. Few were in a position to comply with these exactions, and I saw my opportunity. I took advantage of it, and that was the beginning of my success."[56]

This simple account of the favourable conditions resulting from the Civil War in the United States says nothing of other decisive elements that were advantageous to the young manufacturer. Among these should be mentioned the change of Canada West and Ontario from the agricultural stage to a growing industrialization, and the increase in population. The completion of the railway, particularly the Grand Trunk Railway from Toronto to Montreal in 1856 and its extension to Quebec and Sarnia in 1860, ensured faster production and trade. The Reciprocity Treaty of 1854 restricted the import of some manufactured products, and in 1858-1859 increased duties on finished goods from the United States presented an opportunity for products made in Canada to replace some imports.

And there were other factors that helped R.S. Williams and other Canadian makers to establish their independent factories in the late 1850s. *The Comparative Statement of the Imports at the Port of Toronto* during the years 1854 indicates some of the circumstances that contributed to the successful start of R.S. Williams' business. This statement shows that musical instruments were among the articles subject to 12.5 percent duty and that, in the year 1854, the duty paid for imported musical instruments amounted to some £20,465.[57] Thus the total monetary value of these instruments would have been about £163,000. Although not all instruments imported were melodeons and pianofortes, the average contemporary price of the latter imported instruments (about £250) indicates that approximately 500 were keyboard instruments, the manufacture of which in Canada was very slight in comparison with the States. In the next year the amount of duty, a total of £15,626, indicates that the number of musical instruments imported was lower, as the duty rate remained at 12.5 percent. To the extent that the 12.5 percent duty made the price of instruments produced in Canada lower, it would have been an important stimulant to sales.

From the beginning of R.S. Williams' business, his financial records show an almost uninterrupted growth.[58]

This must have been the consequence of his enlarging both the manufacturing and the trade aspects of his business. These records, as well as the official ones that show the premises occupied by his firm, show that R.S. Williams made these changes in a relatively short time.

"By 1865 the business had so largely increased that Mr. Williams found it necessary to make considerable addition to his premises and to find a separate factory, sash, case and wood department, which he located at 21 Hayter Street, in a two-storey building 60 x 80 feet. These premises he enlarged in 1868 by increasing the length 58 feet and adding another storey. With this large factory he was enabled to extend the field of his operation."[59]

It seems that in the 1860s nothing could prevent R.S. Williams from achieving his prominent position in the musical instrument business. Later biographical information indicates that his success in business was facilitated by qualities that were inextricable from his dedication to his profession and the love of his family. In 1863 Williams' wife, Sarah, gave birth to another son, christened Richard after his grandfather. But the family's joy was short lived; the little son died the same year. Five years later, Williams' daughter Henrietta suddenly became ill and also died.

Despite these sad events, which much have struck him and his family deeply, R.S. Williams continued in his successful business and was, by 1868, contemplating the expansion of his operations to include the production of pianofortes. He was even considering the possibility of a partnership. In 1870 Williams did take a partner. In the records of the Department of the Provincial Secretary, Business Partnerships pre-1900, a partnership was listed with the names of R.S. Williams and William Morris, on June 24, 1870, and it was called "R.S. Williams & Co." The Williamses must initially have been delighted with what seemed a promising move, but the arrangement did not work well, and the whole affair ended when R.S. Williams paid his partner a large bonus to "retire."

The plan to augment the manufacture of melodeons and cabinet organs with the building of pianofortes was shaken but not stopped. Williams' conviction that finding a trustworthy partner outside the family would be difficult had, however, been confirmed. He now looked forward to seeing his eldest child, Robert, in that position as soon as possible.

Robert was at that time a student at Upper Canada College, in the building which had been erected in 1830.[60] Robert's school was in Russell Square, quite close to the Williamses' home. Although the school's curriculum had been subject to lengthy discussion and debate since its establishment, a contemporary document shows what was expected of Robert when he finished school. Edward Mahon, one of Lieutenant Governor Brock's civil secretaries, in his letter to the petitioners in the dispute, wrote

"I am directed by the Lieut. Governor to aquaint you, in reply to your memorial. ... I am also to mention that a boy who is admitted to the College at nine or ten years of age, with industry can certainly qualify himself to enter most professions before he is seventeen, and that he will leave School a Classical Scholar and a good Mathematician, with a critical knowledge of two modern languages, while at the same time, he will find that his commercial education has not been neglected."[61]

With such an education, Robert Williams stood a good chance of becoming the business partner his father was waiting for.

Shortly after his partnership with Morris failed, R.S. Williams enlarged his factory by adding to it a five-storey building, and moved his workshop to the Hayter Street premises, retaining the store at 143 Yonge Street as a warehouse and showrooms.[62] Williams was again influenced by developments in the United States, in this case the rapidly growing piano industry. He prepared, with this move to larger premises, for the next stage in the expansion of his business, the production of pianofortes.

4

THE PIANO INDUSTRY (1872-1880)

The eve of R.S. Williams' piano manufacture; the Canada Organ and Piano Co.; the family business, R.S. Williams & Son.

Was it all to be as simple as the young Canadian manufacturer had imagined? Although he was a successful reed organ producer, his involvement in piano building would receive less support than his special skill in building melodeons and cabinet organs. While the manufacture of free-reed keyboard instruments began only in the second decade of the nineteenth century, the making of pianofortes had a tradition going back to the earliest successful instrument made by Bartolommeo Christophori in Italy between 1689 and the 1720s.[63] Gottfried Silbermann in Freiburg, Germany, made a similar instrument of winged harpsichord form after the description of Christophori's *gravicembali col piano e forte* was translated into German in 1725. In 1758-1760, Christian Ernst Friederici, Silbermann's famous apprentice, constructed the little "square" piano which became popular in Germany. It retained the general clavichord form and construction, but it had a stronger frame, metal strings, and a hammer action.

Johann Christoph Zumpe, an apprentice of Silbermann who arrived in London in 1760, contributed to the popularization of the square piano. After being briefly employed by the Swiss harpsichord maker Shudi, Zumpe began the manufacture of square pianos in London. He met with great success, not only in England but in France where they became the much-favoured "pianos anglais."

The attempts of piano makers to domesticate the piano can be seen in the various forms of upright pianofortes. The wing-shaped instrument with its case on a stand followed the pyramidal shape of the vertically set soundboard, which also led to the peculiar giraffe or harp shape, and the cabinet shape. From these shapes, the tendency was to telescope the instrument to match the scale of a house. Forms known as pianino, cottage or semi-cottage piano, together with other small instruments, were developed. Many manufacturers of the late eighteenth and early nineteenth centuries pioneered refinements of the upright piano just prior to the time when R.S. Williams began his involvement in the piano-making business.

In the early American piano industry, however, the square pianoforte remained the chief product; up to 1866, ninety-seven percent of the annual output of pianos consisted of squares.[64] Only after the appearance of the upright piano at the Paris Exhibition of 1867 did the leading manufacturers in America begin production of the form, adopting the system of the over-strung scale and the full iron frame. The first truly adequate upright, which became the basic pattern for all later instruments of the type, was constructed by Steinway & Sons in New York in 1863. In it, the bass strings crossed the others over one soundboard; the bridges were put nearer its centre so that the setting greatly intensified the tone. The upright piano, as an instrument of a size suitable for a room in an apartment or a house, gained great popularity in Europe as well as in America. The fact that the upright was priced lower than other types of pianos contributed to its success; however, the instrument remained inferior in tone and touch to the best square piano, not to mention the grand or forte piano.

After a grand with a one-piece cast-iron frame was displayed by Chickering of Boston at the 1851 Exhibition,[65] there were many inventions designed to reinforce the frame, until in 1859 Steinway & Sons patented the cast frame over-strung grand piano in America. Since then, the American system of piano construction has influenced the piano producers of the world, who have kept an eye on the rivalry between the leading American firms of Chickering and Steinway.

This brief outline of the development of the piano up to the late 1860s and early 1870s, when R.S. Williams planned to start making pianos, would not be complete without some notes on the production, trade, and other aspects of the piano manufacturing business on the American continent.

After the Civil War the American piano manufacturers had expanded rapidly, and

"a distinctive feature of the piano's widening market in America was the extent to which it was preceded by the harmonium. ... Annual production of these cheap reed instruments exceeded 15,000 by the mid-sixties."[66]

In 1860 there were 110 piano manufacturing firms in the U.S.A. with a labour force of 3,000 making an estimated 20,000 pianos with a value of five million dollars each year. One decade later there were forty-six more firms with a labour force of 4,000 and an annual output of 24,000 pianos with a value of eight million dollars.[67] This rapid growth was largely the result of changes in the organization of production and trade in the American piano industry.

In 1855 the typical factory for piano and harmonium manufacture was "a building similar to an English cotton mill...with steam engines and special machinery applied to the production of every part."[68] The next decades saw increasing specialization as different parts of the instruments were manufactured separately. The well-stocked lumberyard remained a necessity: power-driven machinery supplied the piano makers with selected boards or planks sawed to the thickness and length required. The manufacture of veneers was improved with faster automatic saws, planes, and other such tools. Soundboards were also produced of sawn lumber. Many of the American soundboard manufacturers added ribs, bridges, wrest planks, and complete backs for the upright piano to the production.[69]

The industrial production of hammers began in America when Frederick Matushek of New York invented the hammer-covering machine in 1850. Iron wire was being made for other musical instruments as early as 1351; piano wire made of cast steel dominated the market after it was brought out by Webster and Horsfall of Birmingham in 1845. The production of piano actions was one of the first auxiliary industries. A high degree of automation was possible in the American industry because almost all of the piano makers used the same model of action.

By the second half of the nineteenth century, the piano-case industry contributed significantly to the production of a better commercial instrument, compiled from various ready-made parts; manufacture of cases by the piano maker with limited production would have been unprofitable and sometimes impossible. Thus suppliers of piano cases, like the other branches of the industry, made possible the production of reliable instruments at a price affordable to the average buyer.

When R.S. Williams was preparing to start a piano manufacture of his own, piano manufacture in Canada was modest in comparison with the development in the States. The favourable conditions of transport between Britain and Canada made cities such as Halifax, Saint John, Quebec, and Montreal the first centres of the piano trade, which soon grew not only with the flourishing of imports, but also with the establishment of local manufacturers. Piano manufacture showed promising growth in Lower Canada. Nevertheless, the number of musical-instrument manufacturers who made the piano popular was relatively small, though these few were surprisingly active. The organ builder Samuel R. Warren of Montreal, who established his business in 1836, was one of the earliest known makers of pianos; he later became one of the leading personalities in the pipe-organ industry. To the list of the earliest piano manufacturing firms in Canada outside Toronto should be added John Herbert, George Milligan, George H. Mead, and T.D. Hood, all of Montreal; Laurilliard in Saint John; and Richard Owen in Quebec. H.&J. Philips of Halifax built their first piano in about 1846 for Lieutenant Governor Sir John Harvey.[70] John Herbert represented Canada at the Great Exhibition in London in 1851 with a pianoforte of six and three-quarters octave ompass, from C to G. The other "Canadian" piano at this exhibition was from Nova Scotia, "in a case of bird's eye maple;"[71] it can be tentatively assumed that the maker was the firm of H.&J. Philips.

The early piano makers of Canada were also inventive. The list of Canadian patents registered between 1824 and 1872 includes 4,969 patents, of which twenty-one are concerned with musical instruments and music in general. Thirteen of these are for improvements to the piano, one for improvements to the reed organ, and one for improvements to pipe-organ construction.[72] (See Appendix A.)

The list of patents also reveals more specific information; for example, that the first Canadian patent in connection with pianofortes was granted in 1849 to John Morgan Thomas and Alexander Smith of Toronto.[73] The name Thomas and the year suggest that this is the firm John Thomas & Son, Pianoforte Manufacturers, established in 1832 in Toronto.[74] This firm was one of the earliest in Canada to make pianos: in the *Hamilton Daily Spectator and Journal of*

Commerce, March 13, 1857, an advertisement introduced "Charles L. Thomas, late of the firm of John Thomas & Son, Piano Manufacturers, Toronto, the oldest establishment of its kind in C.W. [Canada West]"; it was also known that "the first piano to be made in Toronto came from the shop of J. Thomas in 1847."[75]

According to R.E. Harding, the patent issued to Thomas and Smith concerned an iron frame. This improvement in the construction of pianofortes

> "consisted of a metal plate screwed upon the wrest-pin block. This plate was attached to the common metal hitch-pin plate. A metal bar, which ran parallel to the lowest string, complemented this frame which was clearly intended for a square pianoforte."[76]

A patent given to Samuel R. Warren of Montreal five years later also became the subject of scholarly evaluation:

> "Samuel Warren, a native of Montreal, Canada, designed a mechanism in which "any numbers of keys or hammers were connected together by coupling levers, so that the striking of any one key should, by means of the coupling level [sic], strike the note of its octave." This coupling was so arranged that the parts striking the octave could be thrown out of action at pleasure, by means of pedal."[77]

George Hooper Mead of Montreal made a contribution to the tuning of the pianoforte, and his "slow-motion wrest pin" secured him Canadian patent No. 306 in 1851.[78]

Although no such activities on the part of R.S. Williams can be traced in the sources, when the new pattern of piano manufacture began he was ready to participate. His experience and skill in the organization and maintenance of the reed-organ industry as well as his basic practical knowledge about the piano would have enabled him to start a new branch of his business much earlier had it not been for shortage of money. The need for capital probably had been the reason for his first, unsuccessful attempt to enter into a partnership. Around this time news of the tremendous success being experienced by Joseph P. Hale of New York must have come to the attention of the Williamses. Hale, who knew nothing at all about piano construction or indeed about musical instruments, had behind him only the money that he had made in the crockery trade. But agents trading between Canada and the U.S. brought fantastic accounts of this self-made man whose system of manufacture and merchandising was hitherto unknown in the American piano trade. For him the piano was a strictly commercial proposition, and all his calculations were aimed at the key question of how to reduce the price of the instrument by reducing the cost of the case, the plate, and the action, the cost of labour and other components. Hale was able to buy all of the parts and assemble them without the risk of losing money that came with investing in machinery for the production of parts. He was also able to select the supplier with the lowest price for each part.

Hale's method of dividing labour into its smallest parts enabled him to reduce labour costs to less than half

Melodeon with iron-cast trestle ascribed to R.S. Williams. R.O.M.

those of his competitors, and he could sell his pianos far below the cost price of a high-grade piano and still make a good profit. In construction and merchandising he was unhampered by tradition, and he became the first American piano manufacturer to discard the agency system: his pianos were sold anywhere to anyone able to pay for them.

It is natural to suppose that such innovations attracted attention in the musical-instrument business. Williams may well have discussed the news with his son and with his foreman, James Coleman, a native of the Isle of Wight who came to Canada in 1848 and settled in Toronto in 1851. Coleman was a friend of Williams, and as a skilled carpenter and builder he was of great assistance to the manufacturer in expanding the premises and making better use of space.[79] Although R.S. Williams adopted some of Hale's practices in an attempt to economize on the production of melodeons and cabinet organs, he still had to wrestle with the problem of how to manufacture a piano which would, like his reed organ, represent a good instrument affordable to working people. His position was quite different from that of Hale. Canada, unlike the United States in 1870, had no manufacturers of piano components and supplies. The only help in this regard came from the Phoenix Foundry of Toronto, which advertised "Castings for Piano-Fortes, Melodeons, sewing machines, etc."[80] These products were known mostly from the cast lyres of reed organs, and from an example of a cast-iron trestle stand of a melodeon attributed to R.S. Williams. If the melodeon, which was unsuccessful, is actually the work of the R.S.W. Company, it can be interpreted as R.S. Williams' attempt to follow the example of Hale in the piano industry. (The idea of a cast-iron melodeon trestle stand was never successfully realized.)

The Canadian piano makers relied on accessories they produced themselves or imported from the States. The construction of a piano was complicated, and a variety of skilled specialists worked on each part and every operation. The advantages of using ready-made parts must have been clear to R.S. Williams; it would have enabled him to eliminate nearly two thirds of the approximately forty-two different workers usually responsible for building a piano.[81] If he bought the keyboards, actions, and hardware as well as the cast frame, he would save the salaries of about fifteen of his usual thirty-eight workmen, all specialists and all well paid. By buying ready-made cases, soundboards and strings, another six workmen could be spared, and the necessary labour force would shrink to about seventeen in all.[82]

Whatever the outcome of such calculations and plans, R.S. Williams would not sacrifice the quality of the instruments that had resulted in his good reputation among manufacturers and customers. He did not intend to throw away what he had put together through years of devoted and industrious work. He would never give up his well-organized workshops that produced the fine cases for the smaller keyboard instruments. He could not give up his skilled workers, who could duplicate the cases, legs, and lyres that he saw on the pianos imported from the States or shipped from Britain and France. In short, R.S. Williams was hampered by an instrument maker's sense of responsibility to his name and to the traditions of his craft, merits unknown to an entrepreneur like Hale who established a business to manufacture pianos "as he would have manufactured bedsteads."[83]

Construction of the piano is more exacting than that of the organ, in that the quality of a piano's sound depends on the resonance of the wood making up the soundboard and the case. Moreover, Canadian weather demands stable woods that will withstand the vast variations in temperature and humidity without losing this resonance. Canadian wood proved to be more suitable than any other for the construction of Canadian keyboard instruments. John W. Herbert, the Montreal piano maker, wrote about the superiority of Canadian woods used in building the piano he exhibited at the Great Exhibition of 1851.

"The case is made of free grain black walnut-tree, veneered with crotch of the same wood; the top and bottom blocks of hard Canadian maple, sounding board of Canadian spruce, which the exhibitor, by experience, is enabled confidently to state is stronger grained and superior for sound to the European wood so generally in use. The ornamental carvings are emblematic of Canada."[84]

The sorts of woods mentioned by Herbert were well represented at the Great Exhibition; black walnut was introduced as

"affording ornamental material for furniture and house building, and is much used in Canada and United States. The chief growth is in the Western part of the Province from which it is imported largely to the United States. ... The bass or white wood...is much used in the manufacture of pianos, and for the inferior of cabinet work."[85]

It is quite natural to expect that the developing piano industry in the United States and Canada would have used local resources of wood, which were of even better quality than European woods, though less good than the exotic imported woods like mahogany, rosewood and sycamore. Williams' woodworking was done exclusively in his new factory, which from the beginning used the superb Canadian wood for most of its products.

Another reason that R.S. Williams could not model his piano-making business on Hale's was that he was short of the capital required to purchase parts from the supplies industry. Williams therefore proceeded according to his traditional methods of construction, the methods he had established to mark business under the sign of the Big Fiddle with tradition and dedication. His first individually made square pianos appeared, showing the new direction in the nature of the business. They were of reliable musical quality; the workmanship revealed the skill of the craftsmen involved.

In the early months of 1873, R.S. Williams began preliminary talks with some Toronto businessmen interested in organ and piano manufacturing on a larger scale. He realized that to establish such an industry he would have to share operational expenses with responsible people, and he managed to generate interest in such an enterprise. On March 17, 1873, their negotiations were interrupted by a long-awaited happy family event, the birth to Sarah and R.S. Williams of another son, who was given the name of his father, Richard Sugden. Robert was then nineteen and Anne fifteen. The good health of Sarah and their baby son allowed R.S. Williams to continue the important meetings with the potential members of the company he planned to direct.

Exactly six month after the birth of Richard Sugden Williams Jr., on September 17, the deal was closed. R.S. Williams signed the Letters Patent with James McGee, Marshall S. Bancroft, William Williams, Daniel Bell, John M. Might, W.M. Baird, John M. Miller, and William McLean; the new firm, the Canada Organ and Piano Co., was established.[86]

The Williamses' wholesale and retail trade continued successfully at the

Richard Sugden Williams Jr., three years old. Courtesy Mrs. I.W. Brock, b. Williams, Toronto.

Yonge Street establishment, and it seemed that the Canada Organ and Piano Co. would be the beginning of significant growth in Canada's piano industry. R.S. Williams' desire to become the director of such a company was realized, too; in the Toronto Directory for the year 1874 he is listed as a "dealer in pianos and organs and managing director Canada Organ and Piano Co." His name is among the piano builders in the Business Directory in the same book. Under the heading "Organs & Pianos" in this Directory is the "Canada Organ and Piano Co." on Hayter Street, with R.S. Williams named as president; however, Williams' name does not appear in the list of "Musical instruments and music dealers." Under "Organ Builders" is listed only one name.[87]

In the directory of the next year, 1875, R.S. Williams is listed only as a piano importer.[88] This was the year in which his second attempt at business partnership met with failure. As for the Canada Organ and Piano Co., "in less than two years this company failed, involving Mr. Williams in heavy losses."[89] Yet the misfortune discouraged neither Williams nor his son Robert, both of whom expended much energy trying to balance the expenses of the Yonge Street and Hayter Street establishments so that they could resume the production of reed organs and pianos. It meant years of hard work in what must have been an atmosphere of considerable tension.

In 1876 another son was born to Richard Sugden and Sarah Williams; he was named Herbert DeMain Williams, after Sarah's mother's family. Williams' daughter Anne was then engaged to Dr. William Moore, a Toronto physician. Robert was engaged to Mazo Thwaite, the daughter of Metcalf Thwaite, a member of the distinguished firm of Fitch, Eby and Thwaite, wholesale grocers in Toronto.[90] The marriage of Robert and Mazo in 1877 secured a good relationship between the two families.

The newly-wed couple settled at 49 Isabella Street. In 1878 Robert Williams is listed as a salesman, while his father remains as a piano and organ dealer. In the same year the father's name appears again in the Business Directory section under the heading "Pianos, Organs, etc."[91] Even from this scanty information it can be assumed that while sales operations were maintained by Robert, the struggle to resume production was entirely in the hands of R.S. Williams. His efforts proved successful; in 1880 Robert was admitted to partnership and the firm of R.S. Williams and Son was established.[92] The Directory of the City of Toronto for 1880 lists Robert Williams as a piano manufacturer.[93]

The directory gives an indication of the objectives of the firm. Another source describes a new and important era in the life of the business:

"They rebuilt the factory, replacing the old one with a fine brick structure. ... The new factory was fitted with every modern appliance, at an expense of upwards of $35,000.00 and the firm entered with renewed energy into the manufactory of pianos. The best skill of the continent was employed, and soon the R.S. Williams' were very favourably known all over Canada.[94]

This information, however, raised some questions about the sudden financial viability of a firm so recently involved in losses through two unsuccessful attempts to secure outside financial support. No explanation is given, but the position of Robert as co-owner of the firm shortly after his marriage to the daughter of a renowned Toronto businessman suggests that perhaps some financial help came from the new relationship between the Williams and Thwaite families.

The eventual success of the Williams firm was representative of how the country as a whole met the challenges at the time. After 1867, renewed prosperity in the Canadian economy resulted from the new Dominion status that united the country in a federation of provinces, and the practice of self-government mirrored a growing political maturity. Under such circumstances there seemed likely a rapid increase in Canada's population, which in the year of Confederation was only three-and-a-half million, and this promised better conditions for industry and marketing.

Great development in material wealth in Ontario, through the vital commercial movement and the growth of technology, made the City of Toronto a significant juncture of commerce and trade for the whole Dominion. Along with this commercial development came the process of cultural growth. A renaissance of interest in music was begun when the Toronto Philharmonic Society was revived in 1872 by James P. Clarke and the Reverend John McCaul, leading personalities in the early musical life of the city. In 1873, Frederick H. Torrington took over the musical leadership of the Philharmonic Society from the retiring Clarke. The arrival in Toronto of professionals such as Edward Fisher (1848-1913), Arthur Elwell Fisher (b. 1848), and the bandmaster John Bayley (c. 1847-1910), to mention a few, influenced the growth of interest in music in the city and laid the cornerstone for future development.

As he began to recover from the second failure in his attempt to succeed in a partnership, then, R.S. Williams was in a position to benefit from the improving financial climate and the political stability resulting from Confederation. He was also well placed in the manufacture, import, and trade of musical instruments to take advantage of a resurgence of interest in music among the citizens of Toronto.

5

ONE THOUSAND PIANOS PER YEAR (1880-1887)

Williams pianos on the North American piano market; introduction of R.S. Williams Jr., to the business

Within a year of its establishment, R.S. Williams and Son was fully representing its pianos in the trade. The New York Piano Company, a "general wholesale and retail house for the disposal of American, Canadian and European High Class Pianos and organs in British North America,"[95] includes R.S. Williams and Son in the group of Canadian piano and organ manufacturers it represents in its 1881-1882 catalogue.[96] Such a listing indicates that as the piano industry and trade developed in Canada, Toronto firms in general and the Williams company in particular participated in its growth.

The New York Piano Company catalogue, like other catalogues and advertising material of Canadian firms at the time, also reveals the continuing public interest in the reed organ; over three decades this instrument had a special social function in Canadian religious and domestic life, especially in small towns and villages, and in rural households. Its usefulness in popularizing music, directly or indirectly, is clear; not only were hymns and songs accompanied by it, but polkas, waltzes, marches, and simple arrangements of opera airs were added to the repertory, as can be seen in *Carhart's Melodeon Instructor*, published in 1851.[97] What becomes apparent, however, is that the organ remained the "little country cousin" of the piano, which had become more fashionable, gradually replacing the reed organ in social function. Another trend that is evident at this time is the rapidity with which revolutionary new methods of the piano industry had spread to Canada, keeping pace with economic development and the public's interest in purchasing pianos.

Piano histories as well as social studies on the piano naturally put Canada among the class of smaller nations adjacent to, and influenced by, the leading countries in the piano industry. As England, France, and Germany were to countries like Holland, Belgium, and Switzerland, so was the United States of America to Canada. As Canada rapidly became a modern and prosperous country, her well-to-do citizens gradually came to give the piano a place of importance in their homes. The manufacture and trade of pianos in Canada, therefore, quickly followed the business in the U.S.

In 1881, about one decade after the establishment of the commercial piano trade in Canada, the catalogue of the New York Piano Company lists Canadian piano manufacturers along with Hale, Albert Weber, and Decker & Son of New York, and Vose & Sons of Boston.[98] The

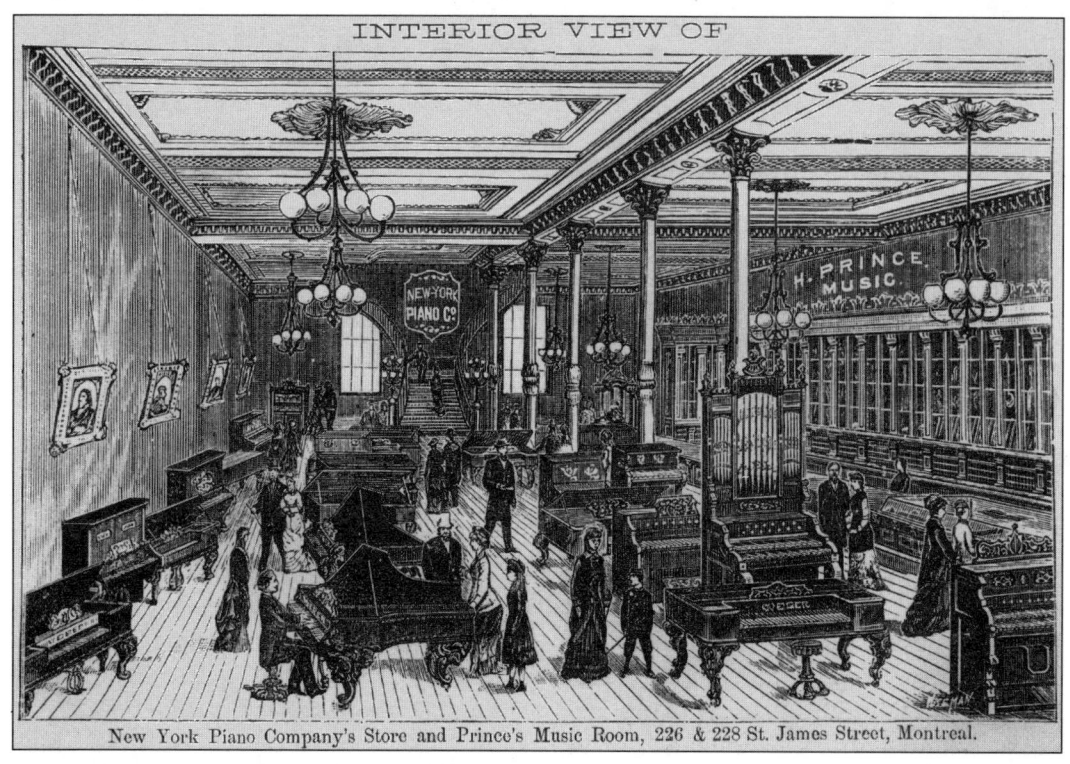

New York Piano Company's Store and Prince's Music Room, 226 & 228 St. James Street, Montreal.

New York Piano Co.'s Music Room at Montreal from the Company's Catalogue and Price List. Courtesy National Library of Canada, Music Division, Ottawa.

biggest challenge to R.S. Williams and his son represented in this catalogue came from a Canadian colleague, Theodore August Heintzmann (later Heintzman), who had been producing pianos of high quality since the establishment of the firm Heintzman & Co. in Toronto in 1866. As R.S. Williams mastered reed-organ building, actually helping to establish the Canadian industry, Theodore A. Heintzman contributed to the successful development of the piano industry in Canada. He had an expert's dedication and determination not to spoil his name with instruments of lower quality.

The Williamses, therefore, faced strong competition in their new line of production, as is clearly indicated by the New York Piano Company catalogue. The Weber merchandise includes the Weber Small Grand Piano (described as the "American Baby Grand"), squares, uprights, and large parlour and concert grands, and is advertised on five pages; Decker's merchandise takes four pages; the pianos of Hale, the New York Piano Company, Vose, Williams, and Heintzman account for two pages each. There is no lack of hackneyed phrases and claims of excellence: "They are especially noted for their prolonged singing qualities, great depth and purity of tone, prompt elastic touch, combined with great power...."; "Owing to the great solidity of construction and improved wrest plank, we claim that these instruments will remain in tune and up to pitch longer than others."

Of Hale's products, the catalogue

offers three different styles of square piano and three upright pianos. The New York Piano Company, located in New York and Montreal, advertises three styles of square and one style of upright piano without any introduction. The preamble for Vose & Sons includes this text:

"These deservedly popular instruments have been before the public over twenty-five years. Thousands of them have been sold in this Dominion. They are used by many of the leading families of Montreal, and have given general satisfaction."[99]

Although the number of pianos sold in Canada is exaggerated here, the information adds to our knowledge of the import of instruments from the United States. Four styles of square and two styles of upright pianos by Vose are listed. The introduction to R.S. Williams and Son reads:

"The pianos of this firm are justly celebrated for their excellent tone and workmanship. They are supplied with the celebrated New York repeating action, and give entire satisfaction. N.Y. Piano Co. are the Wholesale Agents for the Province of Quebec."[100]

Offered are three styles of square and two of upright pianos. Heintzman & Co., Toronto, has no preamble; the catalogue offers five styles of square piano, two styles of upright, and one style of parlour grand.[101]

The styles, descriptions, and prices in this catalogue reveal a few surprises. The Williams pianos are offered at the

Square piano and upright piano by R.S. Williams and Son in the New York Piano Co.'s Catalogue and Price List for 1881-2. Courtesy National Library of Canada, Music Division, Ottawa.

lowest prices; only in the case of the upright are they equal to the prices of Hale's instruments, which in their turn are priced considerably lower than the products of other firms in the catalogue. For example, the seven styles of Weber square pianos are priced from $550 to $880. At this time, Decker & Son prices square pianos from $450 to $550; Hale from $325 to $375; Vose & Sons from $375 to $500; R.S. Williams and Son from $300 to $400; the New York Piano Company from $325 to $375; and Heintzman & Co. from $375 to $550.

In 1881, R.S. Williams and his son Robert were in a very different position from that of American manufacturers like Hale. They were not rich; they started manufacturing pianos a decade later than Hale; and they would not jeopardize their good name for the sake of financial success. How they were able to match Hale's prices remain something of a mystery. The Williams pianos were supplied with the "celebrated New York repeating action," and this reveals that the firm had at least in part accepted the new methods of production, which lowered the cost. The description of the Williams' upright piano style No. 8 shows that the choice of supplier for one of the most essential parts, the action, was made with the intention of using the best parts available. The Wessel action came from the firm of Wessel, Nickel & Gross of New York; the men who gave their names to this firm all trained at Steinway & Sons. These highly skilled manufacturers of piano actions gave the firm a position second to none in America; the foremost makers of high-class pianos were among its customers.[102] The first supplier of parts for the piano industry in Toronto was apparently the firm

> "Wagner, Zeidler & Co., key-board manufacturers and dealers in piano and organ materials, factory 59 to 63 Adelaide Street West, offices and warerooms 116 Bay Street. This business was established in 1878 by Carl Zeidler. ... [who] was the first in the Dominion to establish this particular line of business."[103]

"Celebrated" or not, the Williams pianos proved good enough to be offered on the market along with instruments made by firms of worldwide reputation.

The fact that Williams' square and upright pianos appeared as products of the New York Piano Company in the catalogue of that firm raises the question of whether, for some reason, the pianos were subject to the stencil system. Although strencilling was a controversial practice in the piano trade, it was legal to label an instrument with the name of a company that did not produce it. Sometimes, however, stencilling was used in attempts to circumvent the law. Such misuse did occur at that time in Canada:

> "The Canadian tariff schedule specified a valuation for Hale pianos that Hale tried to have lowered. Conniving with a Canadian dealer, he stencilled the strange name of "Thalberg" on a shipment of his instruments. The ultimate buyer, he figured, might recognize the name of the famous pianist and be attracted by the association, whereas an ignorant customs official might well imagine "Thalberg" to be a new and unfamiliar piano manufacturer and would then accept the Canadian dealer's low valuation."[104]

The suspicion that some Williams pianos were stencilled arises from the fact that the catalogue reproductions show pianos of the New York Piano Company to be identical in every detail with pianos seen in wood engravings bearing the name "R.S. Williams & Son, Toronto." All that has been changed in the New York Piano Company instruments is the name of the producer. On the fallboards of both the Williams piano and the New York Piano Co. instrument appears this inscription: "N.Y. Piano Co., New York." The instruments are identical in every detail of the general shape, of the carving of legs and lyre, music rack, and mouldings, and even in the location of the signature of the wood-engraver, Grant, Barefoot & Co. This indicates that the only difference between these and the instruments identified in the catalogue as products of R.S. Williams and Son is the text on the nameboard. The lists of pianos made by Williams and by the New York Piano Company show different prices for identical instruments. The latter's upright piano, described as style No. 4 and priced at $450, could correspond with the Williams upright style No. 8 with a price of $400.

There is no documentation for this apparent business transaction which in one way or the other must have been beneficial to both parties involved; however, this seems to be the first and only time in their career that the Williamses tried the stencil system.

It can be assumed that the new methods of piano production also influenced R.S. Williams' production of reed organs, which he continued as a secondary line of manufacture. In 1881, a new firm appears under the heading "Organ reeds Makers": Newell Organ Reed Co.[105] Augustus Newell had been an apprentice and later master tuner and producer of reeds for R.S. Williams' organ manufacture. He became at this time the head of his own firm, making it the second of the industries auxiliary to organ making in Toronto.

It is probably correct to suppose that the Newell firm emerged as a consequence of Williams' acceptance of the new organization of the piano and organ industries, although to what extent the Williamses were involved in establishing the Newell Organ Reed Co. has not been discovered. In any case, purchasing reeds and other supplies for the production of reed organs would have been more advantageous for Williams than to continue to finance his own special department, particularly when the reed-organ industry in the country was still growing.

The successful start of his piano business inspired R.S. Williams to plan further development. In 1885 the factory at 31-41 Hayter Street was extended; it now measured 40 by 230 feet and was six storeys high. The office and salesrooms remained at 143 Yonge Street and there was also an office in London, Ontario, at 229 Dundas Street. Williams had local agents in other places, and ten travelling salesmen employed, as well as some 150 skilled workmen who turned out about twenty pianos and six organs each week.[106]

Thus a year's production amounted to over one thousand pianos and more than three hundred reed organs. This was higher than the output of the other leading Toronto manufacturers such as the Daniel Bell Organ Company, which made fifteen to eighteen organs each week, or Heintzman & Co., with a weekly production of twelve to fifteen pianos.[107] As much of the import of musical instruments consisted of pianos and piano parts, the growing interest of the Canadian public in pianos can also be seen from the value of imported musical instruments, which in 1885 totalled $369,000, compared with $220,000 in 1869.

Jim Laver, an employee of the firm since 1873 (probably employed first as a handyman) attempted to "put together his memories" when he retired, and wrote several sheets in pencil.[108] Although the events are presented with a lack of coherence, some of the notes have the value of belonging to an eye witness. Fortunately, Laver's notes have been preserved by Isobel Brock, the daughter of R.S. Williams Jr. Laver's recollections about the shipment of goods with the factory horses, and those revealing the production of the Williams workshop, are the most important. He mentions, for example, "making own pianos, squares been made first, later uprights...at that first order for P.E.I. of twenty-four for school parade to station. ... " Remembering another occasion he wrote, "first small grand walnut case shipped to Brampton. I delivered it to farm north of town, shortly afterward a larger size also a sample in black finish was bought by same family for 2 brothers, both placed in same large dining room. ... " Laver also remembered that "90 pianos per month [were] shipped" and that "seven thousand stools were made, the iron feet being replaced by wooden feet ready to assemble." If these recollections of the monthly output of pianos are correct, the production amounted to 1,080 pianos per year, forty more than the number suggested by a contemporary history.[109]

In the late 1870s the residence of R.S. Williams was at 166 Wellesley Street, at the corner of Sherbourne Street, where the family had moved from Carlton Street. The new home was large and grand with an elaborate facade like a miniature castle. It was probably built in the early 1870s, in the contemporary style known as Second Empire, which was favoured in Toronto at that time.[110]

The residence of R.S. Williams at 166 Wellesley, Toronto. Courtesy Mrs. I.W. Brock, b. Williams, Toronto.

The Williams' mansion had a picturesque mansard roof with dormer windows, a turret with a wrought-iron railing, and a portico with a balustraded staircase, above which a balcony was accessible from the second floor rooms. Bay windows added to the charm and reflected the gaiety so typical of Victorian domestic architecture in Toronto. In those days the location of the new residence was almost suburban, although R.S. Williams drove the distance to factory or office on Yonge Street daily, returning sometimes for lunch.

About the new dwelling, Laver wrote, "The new home was getting replenished by a good purchase of American goods sold on Front Street. I took down cheque for some and helped to deliver it to various rooms [of the house] which was at that time one of the best homes on Sherbourne Street."

Interior of the palatial Williams' residence. Courtesy Mrs. I.W. Brock, b. Williams, Toronto.

The mansion became the centre of family life after the birth of Richard Sugden and Sarah's first grandchild, a son born to Mazo and Robert. Little George Arthur was born in 1878, the year his grandparents moved into the new house. The two younger sons, Richard Sugden Jr., and Herbert, were actually brought up in this house. The boys enjoyed occasional rides in the buggy, or even in the factory delivery wagon of which Laver was in charge. The business and personal lives of the Williams' family were very closely aligned at this time: from Laver's reminiscences we know that the Williamses allowed the use of the factory horse for family purposes and that the proprietors of R.S. Williams and Son "had different good ones [horses] which was a delight to drive in those days when roads was free." Laver probably had good experience with horses, because he wrote, "Robert Williams kindly loaned me his driving [horse] or rather a speeder for AOF parade; on my return he sold some to be placed on track at Windsor." It is obvious that Robert Williams was in favour of the entertainment, as Laver continues: "We used Yonge Street as a show place for deal; purchaser flattered by ability as being a good jockey."

The education of the younger sons of R.S. Williams began at the Wellesley Street Public School. Their father endorsed the boys' interest in the business, which gradually changed as they grew older from the childish pleasure of riding in the factory vehicles to a delight in watching the work in the various workshops of the factory. The habit of Richard Sugden Jr., then attending Jarvis Collegiate Institute, of visiting the factory and warerooms after school hours, encouraged his father in considering the boy's future involvement in the business.

"at the age of fifteen years [Richard Sugden Jr.] started out in the city one morning to interview some prospective purchasers of pianos. In this, his maiden effort as a salesman, he was successful, returning with the order of two ladies, sisters, for a piano."[111]

No wonder that such ambition predestined a career in his father's business, which he entered after finishing his collegiate course.

6

THE FAMILY BUSINESS EXPANDS (1888-1899)

Relocation of the piano production to the Oshawa plant; Richard Sugden Williams Jr., as vice-president of the business; the venture into pipe-organ manufacturing.

In 1888 the Williams' firm purchased the extensive Hall Company factory in Oshawa, where they moved their piano works from Toronto in 1889. The opportunity must have appeared very promising to the Williamses because they spent more than $40,000 in adapting the existing facilities to their business. The old buildings, which had been erected by the Oshawa Manufacturing Company in 1852, were thoroughly repaired; they were re-roofed with slate, and new hardwood floors were laid. New buildings were gradually erected on Duke Street (now Richmond Street) in Oshawa, greatly extending the front of the factory and affording the floor space necessary for what was the largest piano works in Canada.[112] The municipality of Oshawa had granted Williams $20,000 in ten annual installments as an inducement to move his plant there; it also granted the Williams firm a fixed taxation of $250 per year for a number of years.[113]

The move to the Oshawa plant marked a new phase of instrument manufacturing for the Williams' firm. Once in Oshawa the Williams' company manufactured its first large church organ, consisting of more than 100 pipes, for a church at Brighton,[114] although there is no mention of its having been installed.

All available sources on the establishment of the Williams' business in Oshawa present it as an industry of pianos and church organs, an entirely new branch of the activities of R.S. Williams and his son Robert in musical-instrument manufacturing.

Although the piano production was relocated to Oshawa, the centre of the business remained in Toronto. The manufacture of guitars, banjos, and other small instruments was added, and it developed into one of the largest branches of the business. Repair workshops for various instruments were established. Violin repairs in particular gradually developed into a unique and well-known service section of the company. The manufacture of organ reeds, then in the hands of Williams' leading worker Augustus Newell, was moved into the Hayter Street workshops.

The reputation of R.S. Williams, Sr., grew with his continuing success. His achievements since the late 1850s showed the wisdom of persevering and confining his attention to his business. One sign of the respect accorded him by his business colleagues in Toronto is the relationship between R.S. Williams and Son and one of the other leading firms, the Nordheimer Piano and Music Company. The Williamses made

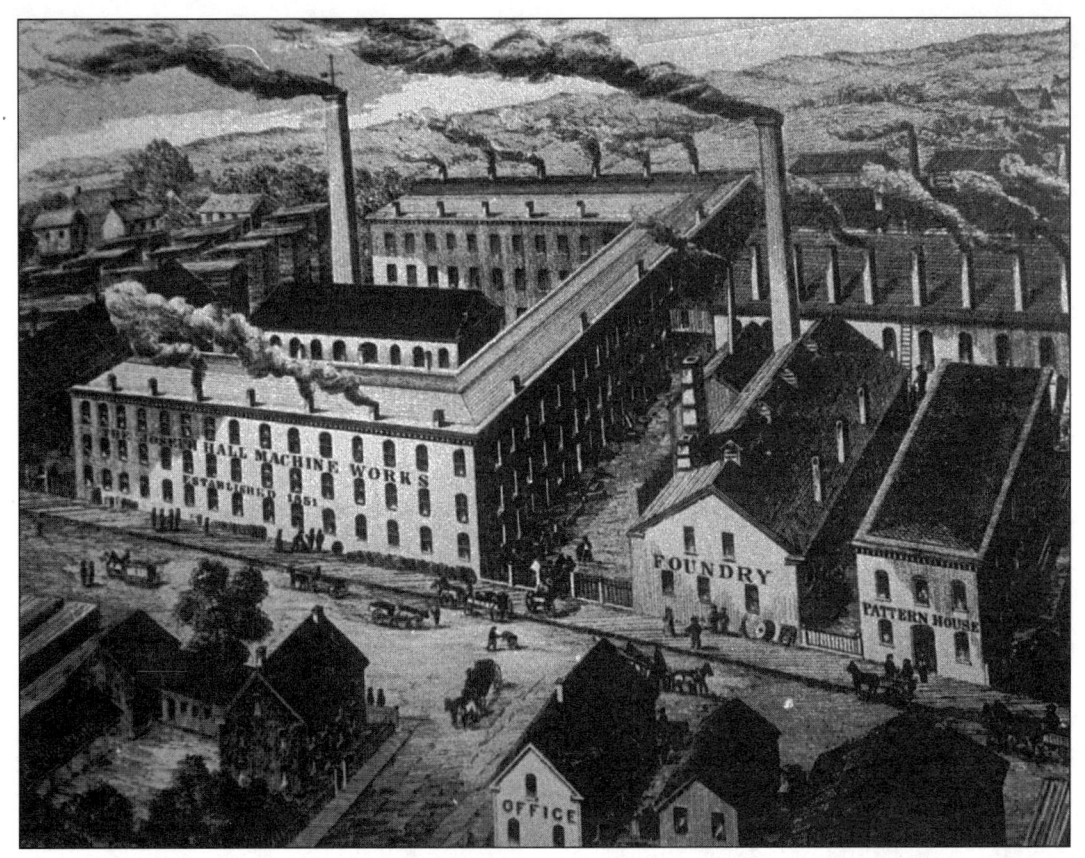

The original plant of the Joseph Hall Machine Works in Oshawa 1870. Courtesy Mr. Th. Bouckley, Oshawa.

uprights for this firm with special text on the fallboard which read, "R.S. Williams & Son, Toronto/ From the Nordheimer Piano & Music Co. Limited." Serial numbers of pianos bearing the names of both companies prove manufacture between 1885 ad 1895.

R.S. Williams' dealings with his customers were marked by an understanding of the musical environment, as described in the memoirs of Williams' employee, Jim Laver. Laver mentions a "Dr." Fisher who, in the early days of his career, was located on St. Joseph Street and rented several pianos from Williams at 143 Yonge Street. When Fisher fell behind with the rent, Laver was sent to look him up but found that he had gone abroad. When later visiting a Mr. Morris, a wholesale grocer and broker on Wellington Street, Laver showed Fisher's bill to Morris. The grocer paused a moment to consider and made the following remarks, which Laver thought were worth remembering: "Do you know who he is? He is a man that is doing a wonderful work for this city among the very best families, and we have to encourage him. So let it rest for the present, and I will see to the settlement on his return." Laver turned in his report and R.S. Williams accepted it. This incident not only gives an indication of Williams' business values, but also hints at the high regard for music and music education in the city.

The address of this Mr. Fisher identifies him as Arthur Elwell Fisher, a promoter of higher music education in Toronto in the 1880s and 1890s. In 1884 he is listed among 131 music teachers in the Toronto City Directory. The popularization of music through teaching experienced continuing growth toward the end of the nineteenth century: the number of music teachers in Toronto had grown to 217 in 1890, and to 260 in 1882. Of these instructors, two founded educational institutions: Edward Fisher, the Toronto Conservatory of Music, and F.H. Torrington, the Toronto College of Music. Undoubtedly the local musical-instrument industry was stimulated by an environment in which musical education was valued. Among the instruments taught, besides piano and violin, were the banjo, guitar, mandolin, and zither. From the testimonials on melodeons and organs in the 1862 and 1864 catalogues, it can be assumed that R.S. Williams had good connections with the music professions in Toronto, and that he benefited from this proliferation of music teachers and schools.

In the last decade of the century the Williams' family reaped some of the fruits of the effort put into the business since its establishment. The musical-instrument industry blossomed with the growing maturity of musical life in Toronto. Despite a certain promiscuity of firms under various branches, presentation of their names and locations helps to reconstruct a clear picture of the musical instrument industry. (See Appendix B.) The clustering of these businesses in one area of the city was a powerful factor in the propagation of music in Toronto at the time.[115] To this picture should be added the relatively strong and growing group of music publishers and dealers.

Within this network of firms competition must have been stiff, even for an important firm like R.S. Williams and Son. On the other hand, at this time Toronto's music culture, and subsequently its music business, was significantly enriched by the opening of a new music hall.

"By the public spirit and generosity of Hart A. Massey, Massey Hall was erected; it was a godsend to musical art. Choristers and soloists deserted with cheerfulness the old Horticultural Building in Allen Gardens, a draughty firetrap, and the opening concerts in the new hall in 1894 under Dr. Torrington's direction were notable."[116]

Also in 1894, the Mendelssohn Choir was founded by Augustus Stephen Vogt (1861-1926), son of a small pipe-organ builder in Preston. Another stage in the education of the Toronto public in the appreciation of fine music had begun.

Under these circumstances the Williamses continued their participation in the musical-instrument industry and trade with all the weight of their long experience and with the respect generated by the father. Robert's children were growing up; in 1892 George Arthur was nearly seventeen, Harold Ernest a year or two younger, and their sister Mabel entering her teens. The happy marriage of Williams' daughter Anne had been broken by the sudden death of her husband, Dr. Moore. They had only one child, a son, William Elwood. Herbert,

London (Ontario) Branch of the R.S. Williams firm in 1890. The figure to the left is Mr. Wm. McPhillips, the well-known London dealer, then with the R.S. Williams House. In the centre is Mr. Croden, manager of the Branch, and his new clerk "Harry" Stanton. Courtesy National Library of Canada, Music Division, Ottawa.

showing an inclination toward administrative matters, was engaged in the office management of the family business, and eventually oversaw the London, Ontario, branch of the firm, R.S. Williams Jr., was showing an ambition to gain the expert knowledge needed for the construction and repair of musical instruments, both old and modern.

R.S. Williams had recognized early the special interest of his younger son, Richard Sugden, Jr., in the business. The young man's fondness for the old instruments that were acquired through trade or were brought in for repair to the offices on Yonge Street was evident. He showed an attitude to the business that was based on a desire to penetrate the secrets of the instruments that had served as models for contemporary ones. At the end of the 1880s, when he joined his father and brother in the firm, a large number of old viols, violins, guitars, lutes, and zithers (made in England under the name English Guitar), as well as some early keyboard instruments, had been acquired by his father. R.S. Williams Jr., was particularly interested in old violins, and under the guidance of his father spent many hours in the fiddle repair workshop, which had been busy since the first days of the business. This period marked the beginning of the son's collecting activities, which were to help make Toronto one of the centres of the world violin trade.

R.S. Williams admired the inventiveness with which his son found his way to knowledge of the construction and repair of musical instruments. Many years later, R.S. Williams Jr., described one of these ways:

"In those early days, Mr. Munro was Head Customs Officer and I had the pleasure of living across the street from him, on the corner of Sherbourne and Wellesley. I made an arrangement with him to check up values for duty purposes of instruments coming through the customs and was fortunate to make a list of any worthwhile instruments. Mr. Bartram, his successor, also worked with me, and we had many funny experiences in trying to stop smuggling. Of all the violins coming into Canada, the greater proportion passed through my hands. This naturally was a great help to me in my profession of violin expert."[117]

The desire to gain more knowledge about the world of music led the young Williams to turn to literature on the subject; books on the history of music, on violins and other instruments, on the lives of great musicians, and on drama and opera, soon filled the firm's library. This line of endeavour also met with his father's approval and enthusiastic support.

On March 27, 1895, Richard Sugden Williams Jr., became vice-president of the newly formed firm, R.S. Williams & Sons Co. Limited.[118] Perhaps this appointment was a grand wedding present: R.S. Williams Jr., was married in Toronto on March 31, 1895 to Alma Coleman, a skilled pianist, daughter of Charles Coleman who was at one time leader of the Philharmonic Society of Toronto.[119]

The new firm was incorporated with capital of $500,000, with R.S. Williams, Sr., as president. His two sons continued their efforts to maintain the firm's prosperity and overcome the tough competition. From these years at the end of the nineteenth century are preserved pipe organs, made in the piano factory in Oshawa, stencilled with the newly adopted name of the firm. Judging from the history of the Williamses' business programme, their building of pipe organs was a rather late attempt to participate in this branch of the musical-instrument industry. It was only an experiment, and production lasted but a few years. Despite the short period of production several Williams pipe organs are even now in practical use, some having been rebuilt. Some, however, were lost forever, discarded in favour of electronic instruments, or destroyed by fire. The few that remain are worthy of being included in our cultural heritage. These organs were relatively small compared with more advanced contemporary instruments; they were based on organs of the type generally known as Baroque or Praetorius.[120]

The Williams pipe organs were furnished with tracker action and worked by mechanical movement, sometimes combined with the pneumatic system to operate the pedals:

"The Methodist church in Calgary, (later Central), got its first pipe organ about 1889 with the erection of its brick church on Second Street

R.S. Williams Jr., c. 1895. Courtesy Mrs. I.W. Brock, b. Williams, Toronto.

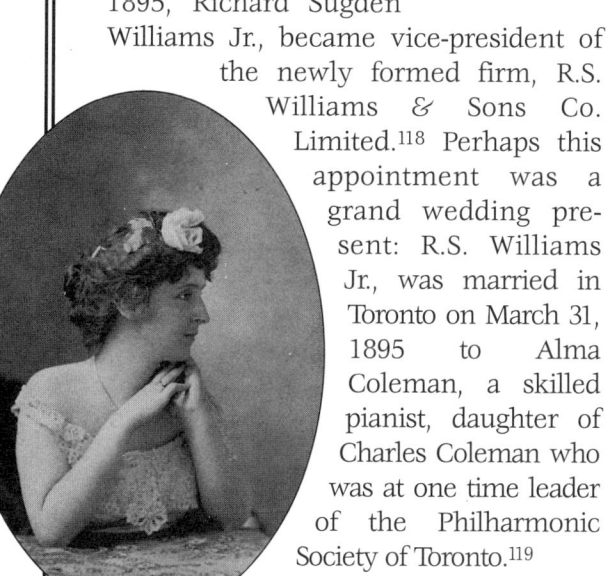

Miss Alma Coleman, c.1895. Courtesy Mrs. I.W. Brock, b. Williams, Toronto.

53

[Advertisement: The R. S. WILLIAMS & SONS CO. LIMITED, MANUFACTURERS OF HIGH-CLASS PIANOS And STRINGED INSTRUMENTS of all descriptions. Our Special Brands, "THE ECHO" and "ARTIST," are Endorsed by the Profession, and Warranted. Importers and Dealers in MUSICAL MERCHANDISE. CATALOGUES FREE. CANADIAN AGENTS FOR The EDISON PHONOGRAPH, BETTINI MICO-SPEAKER, POLYPHONE ATTACHMENTS, REGINA MUSIC BOXES. Large Stock of Machines and Records to select from. CORRESPONDENCE SOLICITED. WRITE FOR CATALOGUES. FACTORY OSHAWA, ONT. HEAD OFFICE and WAREROOMS 143 Yonge St., TORONTO. The R. S. WILLIAMS & SONS CO., Limited.]

Advertisement with a view of the Oshawa factory before 1902. Courtesy National Library of Canada, Music Division, Ottawa.

West between Fifth and Sixth Avenues. Built by R.S. Williams and Son, Company Limited, of Toronto, it was consigned to an unremembered addressee in "Calgary, N.W.T.", and we are grateful to the memory of one of the organ pumpers for this detail. ... This organ turned out to be most peripatetic, having served in no less than four different church buildings.

Its first location was a recessed loft behind the choir seats in Central Church. Its display pipes, stencilled in blue, gray-blue and gold as was the fashion of the period, dominated the front of the church. ... This organ had the usual tracker action, but it employed the newly invented "tubular pneumatic" type to operate the pedals. Playing an organ in those days was always a two-man proposition. The bellows-boy at the pump handle behind the scenes, did the manual labor, while the organist at the keyboards usually took all the credit.! The "bellows signal" provided their means of communication."[121]

The year of delivery of this organ must have been after the establishment of the R.S. Williams and Son Company plant in Oshawa in 1888; 1890-1891 is probably the correct date, judging from the known organs that have survived that were made by the firm up to the end of the nineteenth century. Even without a certain date of manufacture for the organ, this information is of special value because of its historical and technical details, including the specifications noted (see Appendix C).

Of the Williams' organs in Ontario, the oldest seemed to be the one in St. Margaret's Roman Catholic Church in Midland. This instrument was not accompanied by documents of purchase of delivery, because St. Margaret's Church was not the original purchaser. The church was built in 1912, and the organ appeared to be about twenty-two years older, probably built in the Oshawa plant before R.S. Williams & Sons Co. Limited was established in 1895. It would seem that the original nameboard, with "R.S. Williams and Son, Toronto" on it, was removed and never replaced. Since the Williams' firm bought the Oshawa plant in 1888, and since the repairs and renovation probably slowed down full-time work for some time, piano and organ manufacture there probably began between 1890 and 1895, when the Midland organ was built.

The most valuable information about this instrument comes from its master, the organist Bob Witham:

> "We believe that the organ came to St. Margaret's from St. Mary's Catholic Church on Bathurst Street, Toronto, circa 1912. ... The organ was repaired and refurbished following about fifteen years of inactivity in 1978.
>
> Although there is no nameplate on the organ, we knew it was a Williams organ by the characteristic draw knobs and by the Oboe 8 French double-nut reed of which we believe only one other exists, in the Williams' organ in St. Paul's Church on Power Street, Toronto. Also the Williams stamp was visible on the cast weights of the bellows."[122]

It is clear that Witham's knowledge of, and close attention to, the instrument in his care contributes to the historical appreciation of the church, the organ itself, and the manufacturer of the organ.

Bellow weight from the Midland organ. Courtesy of St. Margaret Roman Catholic Church, Midland, Ontario.

Two manual pipe organ built by R.S. Williams and Son between 1890 and 1895, Midland, Ontario. Courtesy St. Margaret's Roman Catholic Church, Midland, Ontario.

The church and the organ were destroyed by fire on Christmas Eve 1986.

St. Paul's Roman Catholic Church at Queen and Power Streets in Toronto is a beautiful, historic setting for worship and music. It was built by Joseph Connoly in 1887, and in 1889 it was solemnly dedicated.

> "This church was a rather courageous attempt at the design in the Italian Renaissance manner, in a city where nearly all churches were Gothic. ... The interior is quite the most beautiful church interior in Toronto and because of it the church should appear in any list of buildings worthy of preservation."[123]

According to the history of the church, the organ was installed in 1898.

Interior of St. Paul's Roman Catholic Church in Toronto, Queen & Power Streets; with the two manual organ built by Mr. R.S. Williams & Sons Co. Limited in the year 1895, or shortly after. Courtesy of St. Paul's Roman Catholic Church, Toronto, Ontario.

This organ was one of the Williamses' bigger instruments and in 1977, thanks to the church, it underwent a major restoration after nearly a century's good service.

However, St. Paul's was probably the second place where the organ was installed. Gabriel Kney, the renowned organ builder from London, Ontario, restored the organ and discovered several marks inside the case that indicate that it was designed for a "St. Thomas" church. He was not able to find a church called "St. Thomas" in Toronto into which this organ could possibly have fit. In his opinion, another indication that the organ was first designed for a different church is that the centre facade pipes have been shortened at the top to fit into a restricted height. This organ was made in the year 1895 or shortly thereafter, because the nameboard gives the name as "R.S. Williams & Sons Company Ltd., Toronto."

St. John's Anglican Church in Cayuga, Ontario, has a well-preserved organ made by R.S. Williams & Sons. The church was built in 1986, and the organ's case indicates that the instru-

General view of the two manual organ, St. John's Anglican Church, Cayuga, Ontario, in architectural setting of the interior. Courtesy of St. John's Anglican Church, Cayuga, Ontario.

Detail with pedals of the Cayuga organ. Courtesy of St. John's Anglican Church, Cayuga, Ontario.

Two manual Williams' organ, unknown location. Courtesy of Mr. Th. Bouckley, Oshawa.

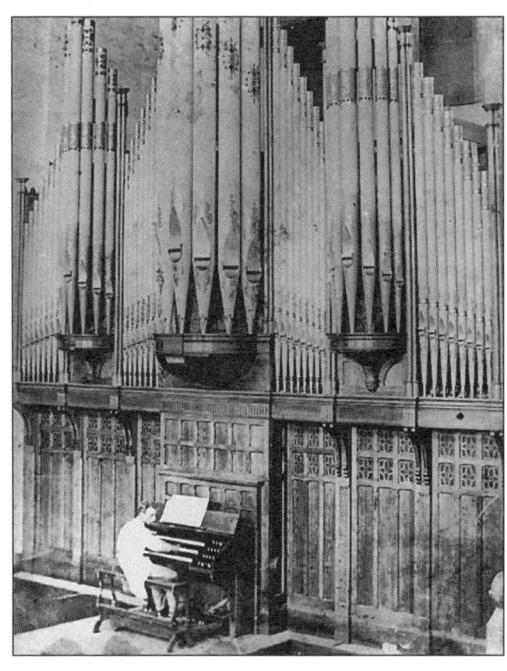

Three manual Williams' organ in the assembly hall being tested by the organist of the Oshawa plant. Courtesy of Mr. Th. Bouckley, Oshawa.

Interior of the workshop and workers in the Oshawa Williams' plant. Courtesy Mr. Th. Bouckley, Oshawa, Ontario.

ment was made towards the end of the last decade of the nineteenth century. This two-manual organ has a mechanical action. It is still in its original state and, according to information from Dubay Organs Ltd. of Burlington, Ontario, which maintains the organ, is in good working condition despite its vintage. They believe that is a typical organ of its era, one which has been preserved extremely well.

Only one of these four R.S. Williams organs was found in its original location. Photographs document more Williams organs that are still unfound. It was the private photographic archives of Thomas Bouckley, the Oshawa historian and author, that gave this unexpected surprise. Among priceless negatives and prints were photographs of organs taken in various churches. Many of the photographs in Bouckley's collection were saved by the devoted collector at the last minute, or were retrieved from the garbage. Among them is a photograph of a three-manual instrument in the west end of the Williams plant in Oshawa, an area built without a second floor to allow for the construction and assembling of these huge pipe organs. The organist is shown during the testing process, seated on a lyre-legged bench identical to those

WILLIAMS PIANO CO EMPLOYEES 1890

Crew of the factory in Oshawa, 1890. Courtesy Mr. Th. Bouckley, Oshawa, Ontario.

in the Midland and Cayuga churches, and in St. Paul's in Toronto.

Among these extremely rare photographs is another taken in the Oshawa workshop during the construction and assembling of organs. Probably both pictures of the plant were taken before 1902; this was the year when the Williams business was divided, the Williams Piano Company Limited was established, and organs ceased to be produced by the company in Toronto or Oshawa.

R.S. Williams, Sr., in the last decade of the nineteenth century, was still fully engaged in the business, in Toronto and all its branches. At the time of the 1899 Western Fair in London, Ontario, he visited the branch of his business there. The *London Free Press* noted the event in a special report. A photo of Williams appeared with the following caption:

"A notable visitor, Mr. R.S. Williams, the famous piano builder,/visits the Western Fair/expresses himself as pleased with/London's Great Show./And chats most entertainingly/on the history of Canadian piano and organ making... – wonderful strides have been made in the development of musical instruments since he began his apprenticeship in 1848 [sic]."The report goes on to describe Williams:"Mr. R.S. Williams, the oldest manufacturer of musical instruments in

Canada, was a visitor to the city yesterday and was the guest of his son, Mr. Bert Williams, the proprietor of the London Branch of the R.S. Williams Company. ... A *Free Press* reporter met Mr. Williams at his son's musical emporium, Dundas Street, last evening, and the grand old gentleman chatted most entertainingly on the evolution of musical instruments in Canada. Mr. Williams is a gentleman of stately appearance and kindly address, and a stranger is at once at home in his presence."[124]

A picture of R.S. Williams in his mid-sixties accompanies the article. Although the reporter describes Williams as a "grand old gentleman," the photograph reveals a rather active individual, a personality conscious of having achieved success through half a century of dedicated work.

Portrait of R.S. Williams with his signature, circa 1895. Courtesy Mrs. I.W. Brock, b. Williams, Toronto, Ontario.

7

THE TURN OF THE CENTURY (1890-1906)

The publication of sheet music, a sideline; the family firm divided into Williams Piano Company Limited and R.S. Williams & Sons Co. Limited; the death of the founder.

The last decade of the century was one of the brightest periods for the Williams' family, both in business and in private life. There were no serious accidents, and no deaths eclipsed the good years R.S. Williams and his wife, Sarah, spent with the families of their children. Richard Sugden Williams Jr., started a family; in 1895 his wife, Alma, gave birth to a baby girl they named Irma.

For the benefit of the entire family, Williams acquired some property in the Toronto beaches. Coach and horses were used to transport the family to the large frame house that became their summer quarters. There, Williams and Sarah often enjoyed lovely days in the late years of their busy lives. In those years, at the turn of the century, R.S. Williams became more and more devoted to his home life; aside from his involvement in the business, his only outside interest was the Aid, Loan and Saving Company of which he was president.[125] In 1900, R.S. Williams, aged sixty-six, was still president of the family business and directed its affairs. With his sons' help he had been able to increase very considerably the amount of business during the preceding few years.

The publishing of music was added to the family business (see Appendix D), but only as a sideline of its other more significant activities. R.S. Williams was involved from the very beginning in selling music and instruction books; however, aside from the production of catalogues the firm was not engaged in publishing until piano manufacture became its chief line of business.

The earliest publication was the popular song "Canada's Welcome," published in 1878, two years before Williams' partnership with his son Robert. Robert Awde's words and Edward Gledhill's triumphant march[126] celebrate the arrival in Canada of John Douglas Campbell, Marquis of Lorne, and his wife Princess Louise. (Campbell was Governor General from 1878 to 1883, and founded the Royal Society of Canada, the Royal Canadian Academy of Arts, and the National Gallery.) The music is written with piano accompaniment. Although it is a piece dedicated to the supreme Canadian official and his wife, the text as well as the music are typical of the marches, dances, and ballads that contemporary publishers preferred to more serious music for commercial reasons.

The next pieces of sheet music published by Williams that have been preserved comprise the Williams Musical Library. The sheets of this series are not dated, but the name of the publisher, R.S. Williams and Son, indicates that the Williams Musical Library began at the same time as this new name (1880). Four of the sheets originate in the period between 1880 and 1895, and four were issued after 1895 when the publisher's name had become R.S. Williams & Sons Co. Limited. Of the eight numbers in the series the first and sixth are missing from the R.S. Williams Collection in the ROM. The "Williams' Piano Schottische," published in the same period, is perhaps No. 1 of the Williams Musical Library; however, instead of the normal heading and serial number, the cover identifies the piece with the title and the claim, "The immense success!" (Since the beginning of the nineteenth century, in the towns of Upper Canada and the Maritimes, tradition had kept Schottisches in favour.)

The publishing activity of manufacturers and dealers in musical instruments served as an important vehicle of advertisement. The covers usually carried direct or indirect information about the publisher's main area of specialization. R.S. Williams also used this approach and, in addition to the title of the piece of music and its author, put good pictures of pianos made by the firm prominently on the covers. The "Williams' Piano Schottische" and the "Ta-ra-ra-boom-der-E Waltz" picture the same upright piano, although on the latter cover the decorative front of the instrument is open. The names of "distinguished Artists using and recommending these High-Class Pianofortes" are identical on both covers, Professor F.H. Torrington being at the top of the list.

62

For No. 3 "Blondina Waltz", and No. 4 "In the Lead," the design of the covers is changed, and shows a Williams grand piano with open lid. Of the changes in the list of names of those who favour Williams pianos, one is significant: under the title "Williams Piano Patrons," it begins with "Her Majesty The Queen, Windsor Castle." The list includes "Rt. Hon. Sir Chas. Tupper, G.C.M.G. – Canada's High Commissioner," "Hon. G.W. Ross, L.L.B. – Minister of Education," and other names from previous lists. Besides the information recorded much later by R.S. Williams Jr. about the two Williams pianos in Windsor Castle, this is the only known contemporary documentation of Royal patronage.

Another important piece of information appears on the cover of No. 4 "In the Lead": besides the advertisement for "High Grade Pianofortes," there is also advertising for "Church Pipe Organs." This indicates that Williams' pipe-organ manufacture probably began with the opening of the Oshawa works in about 1890. The Midland organ mentioned in the previous chapter belongs among the instruments from early in Williams manufacture of pipe organs.

Cover of "Canada's Welcome." Courtesy Metropolitan Toronto Library Board, Toronto, Ontario.
Cover of "Ta-ra-ra-Boom-der-e- Waltz." Courtesy Metropolitan Toronto Library Board, Toronto, Ontario.
Cover of "In the Lead." Courtesy Metropolitan Toronto Library Board, Toronto, Ontario.
Cover of "The Queen City." Courtesy Metropolitan Toronto Library Board, Toronto, Ontario.
Cover of the "Queen's Plate," March and Two-Step. Courtesy National Library of Canada, Music Division, Ottawa, Ontario.

Among the sheet music published by Williams after 1895 is the march "The Queen City," paying homage to the City of Toronto. No. 5 of the Williams Musical Library, it was published probably before 1902 when the firm was again divided and the Williams Piano Company was established in Oshawa. The cover of this piece still has the advertisement for church pipe organs marked with the name R.S. Williams & Sons Co. Ltd. The names of the authors are Wittich, Muir, and Yule: the second probably was Alexander Muir, author of "The Maple Leaf Forever"; and the third J.L. Yule, who was a music teacher and founder of the Owen Sound Registered Music Teachers' Association in 1914.[127]

The next two Williams Musical Library pieces preserved are No. 7 "Black America," a march by H.H. Zickel, and No. 8 "Queen's Plate," a march and two-step by C.M. Vet. The latest piece among those discovered during this recent research is a song by Morris Manley, "The Ottawa Fire," mourning the loss of the Parliament building's central block which was destroyed by fire on February 3, 1916.

The bulk of contemporary music published in Canada consisted of pieces of light or popular music. It is no wonder that sheet music was a byproduct for firms that concentrated on the manufacture and trade of musical instruments; the musical and artistic value of these works, composed by amateurs or

Crew of the factory in Oshawa, inc. 1900. Courtesy Mr. Th. Bouckley, Oshawa, Ontario.

musicians who played this kind of music, was not on a particularly high level. We should, however, recognize the importance of these pieces of sheet music, for "they give, through their titles, texts and cover illustrations, a better reflection of Canadian social history than compositions of more artistic and academic aspiration."[128]

R.S. Williams gave special attention to brass bands. This tradition, first indicated in the earliest preserved catalogue of 1862, grew with the firm, and even in the early twentieth century the Williamses were engaged in publishing music for brass bands. Lieutenant John Slatter (1864-1954), bandmaster, composer, arranger, and editor in Toronto, arranged the band book *National Airs and Regimental Marches*, which was published by R.S. Williams & Sons Co. in 1911. *The Williams' Canadian Patriotic Band Book* was published

Robert Williams, co-founder of the Oshawa Piano Works, c. 1899. Courtesy Mrs. I.W. Brock, b. Williams, Toronto.

George Arthur Williams, secretary-treasurer of the Oshawa factory, in his office, c. 1905-8. Courtesy Mr. Th. Bouckly, Oshawa, Ontario.

The daughters of R.S. Williams Jr., Irma, Madeleine and Isobel. Courtesy Mrs. I.W. Brock, b. Williams, Toronto.

probably a few years later; like the earlier book, it contained "The Maple Leaf Forever" and "O, Canada," and was arranged by John Slatter. Both band books are advertised in Williams catalogue No. 36,[129] disclosing the typical repertory of Canadian band music of the time. At the bottom of the page the *Canadian Bandsman and Orchestra Journal* is offered for subscription at fifty cents a year. This monthly started under the name *Canadian Bandsman and Musician* in June 1913, and was a Williams house publication edited by Alexander L. Robertson (1894-1967). In 1924 Robertson incorporated it into *Musical Canada*, a monthly journal that had been founded in Toronto in 1906. Surprisingly, there is not a word in the written recollections of R.S. Williams Jr., about the publishing of the *Canadian Bandsman and Orchestra Journal*.[130]

In the same catalogue are offered two popular folios: the cover of "Favourite Piano Classics, Vol. 1" is reproduced in the catalogue. As this folio bears the firm's signature, R.S. Williams & Sons Co. Limited, it is obviously part of the Williams' publishing endeavour.

The publishing of music remained, however, a minor aspect of the Williams' business. The success of the business as a whole was marked by events such as expansion into other provinces. Among the news in the musical-instrument trade journals in 1901 is a small article with the title "$100,000 of Pianos":

"That is the amount that Willis & Co. of Montreal, have contracted for from the house of R.S. Williams & Sons Co. Limited...and the Williams piano boom in Quebec Province. ... Mr. Coutourie, head of the piano department of the Williams house, has increased their sales wonderfully in the past two years."[131]

Progress in establishing representation of the firm in eastern Ontario is illustrated in another article in the same issue of the *Canadian Music and Trade Journal*. It reads, "The bulk of the piano and music supply trade of Ottawa is being done by J.L. Orme & Son, while Mr. Bert Williams is doing a land office business with Williams pianos, having ten men on the territory."[132]

By this time Richard Sugden Williams Jr., had attained a level of connoisseurship in the world of musical instruments, aided by his business trips to Europe. This travel experience was especially useful in broadening his knowledge of old violins through contact with makers, collectors, and performers. His expertise as a collector of old violins

Manufacturing guitars and mandolins. Courtesy National Library of Canada, Music Division, Ottawa, Ontario.

Finishing room. Courtesy National Library of Canada, Music Division, Ottawa, Ontario.

Small goods sample room of the Wholesale Department. Courtesy National Library of Canada, Music Division, Ottawa, Ontario.

Piano show and warerooms. Courtesy National Library of Canada, Music Division, Ottawa, Ontario.

proved to be a much better entrée to these circles than his position in the manufacture and trade of violins. Being much younger and open to new experiences on his journeys, he was also more progressive in his views on business than his brother Robert, who preferred a more cautious approach and pursued business goals according to established methods.

The father's decision to let each son work on his own initiative brought about a change in direction that marked the next phase of the family enterprise. In 1902 the business was divided: the Williams Piano Company Limited was founded in Oshawa with a capital of $250,000; the business in Toronto was continued under the old name, retaining an equal capitalization. Robert Williams was made president of the Williams Piano Company. As president of the Toronto business, his father remained actively identified with the firm until 1903, when failing health compelled him to relinquish active control and place it in the hands of his sons.[133]

In 1903 Robert Williams also retired from active management because of ill health. Control of the Oshawa business was assumed by Frederick Bull, who later became its president and managing director. To have a part of the business headed, for the first time, by someone outside the family must have been a bitter pill for the ailing founder. The next year, however, he was given a special gift – the first New Scale grand piano produced in the Oshawa plant.

The following year R.S. Williams, Sr., spent among the flowers and plants in his admirable greenhouse, the conservatory of his beautiful residence at Wellesley and Sherbourne Streets, where

R.S. Williams Sr., with a violin, 1905. Courtesy Mrs. I.W. Brock, b. Wiliams, Toronto, Ontario.

he was still a kindly and hospitable entertainer. His grandchildren were now grown: Robert's son George Arthur was the secretary-treasurer of the Williams Piano Company in Oshawa, where Harold Ernest also worked as a superintendent; their sister Mabel helped her mother. The daughters of Richard Sugden, Jr., were growing very fast, too. Irma was nine, Madeline five; their baby sister Isobel was born in 1905 in the new house built on Cluny Avenue the previous year. Herbert, who had previously been in London, Ontario, was involved in the piano business in Ottawa, and Anne's son William had taken over the recently established Winnipeg branch of the R.S. Williams & Sons Company. The European depot of their business was founded in London, England, at 6 Eldon Street.

It must have been a great occasion when, in 1905, the sons visited their father to show him the thirty-first catalogue of the business he had established forty-nine years before. Page by page, section by section, the catalogue evoked the long journey from small beginnings to successful business. The pictures showed the familiar places – the workshops and storage, the showrooms all neatly arranged, the first-floor piano showrooms at 143 Yonge Street, the retail small goods department, and the retail Edison phonograph department, an innovation brought into the business by R.S. Williams Jr., five years before. In the second-floor piano warehouse was a one-manual pipe organ of chamber size; the small goods sample room of the wholesale department on the same floor had a well-arranged display of hundreds of instruments, parts, and accessories.

Many well-known violin-making firms were now supplying the Williams' business with high quality instruments. August Kneizel of Vienna, François Savois of Paris, Louis Lowendall of Berlin, and Johann Glass of Leipzig were among the European firms represented in the business. In the year 1905, the Williamses sold no fewer than 27,000 violins at prices ranging from $1.50 to $150. A variety of instruments made up this remarkable number, as the preamble to the violin section of the thirty-first catalogue notes:

"We at all times carry a very large and varied stock of Violins in all of the different classes, from the inexpensive German, and good commercial, to the finest instruments of the best modern makers, and rare specimens of the famous old masters. In this catalogue we list and describe only our commercial and high grade new instruments, our Old Violin Collection being fully described in booklet issued by that department."[134]

However, among the pages depicting the "commercial and high grade instruments" are a few pages advertising instruments of the Williams Collection of rare old violins, such as a "Giovan Grancino" valued at $3,000, an "Andreas Guarnerius" valued at $5,000, and a Francesco Ruggeri (sic) for $4,000. The text advertising this collection reads, "Our Collection of Rare Old Violins, Violas and Cellos, is one of the largest and best selected on this continent, and includes instruments ranging in price from thirty dollars up to the thousands."[135]

Hard sell advertising was not shunned, as can be seen in the article introducing the violins of Johann Glass of Leipzig, to which an entire page is devoted. (Glass was a successful copier of the Cremona school of Italian instrument makers.) The article ends with these hints about possible substitutes for the rare and expensive old masterpieces:

"In musical circles the idea prevails that an old Italian instrument is indispensable for the higher art in violin playing; however, these instruments are constantly becoming rarer, and so the question naturally arises whether an old instrument is really such a necessity. Is not a new one perfectly constructed (we are speaking only of the Glass instruments) to be preferred to an old one in bad state of preservation and therefore of questionable value? Formerly the delight of playing a fine instrument was only possible by a considerable expenditure, but to-day there is every opportunity to secure a first class instrument at a moderate price."[136]

The bows, like the violins in this catalogue, originated with various suppliers; one group was marked and apparently made by the Williamses. The lowest price for a bow was seventy-five cents, the highest thirty-five dollars. The makers of high-grade violin bows were Johann Glass of Leipzig and W.E. Hill & Sons of London. According to the catalogue, both firms followed "the general line of the best Tourte bows," probably referring to the bows of François Tourte (1741-1835) of Paris, son of Tourte-Le Pére, the inventor of the modern bow. Some collectors bought gold-mounted bows made by Tourte-Le Fils for two hundred dollars. However, a gold-mounted bow by Glass was offered in this catalogue for thirty-five dollars.

The catalogue was rich in violin models bearing the names of the famous violin makers such as Stradivari, Amati, Maggini, Gasparo da Salo, Guarneri, Stainer, Hopf, and Klotz. Among the "Special Styles" were violins such as "Ole Bull, ebony fingerboard and tailpiece, selected medium grain top, light red, amber shaded, back bears name 'Ole Bull'. Fitted with good quality brass patent heads."[137] There was a "Russian model," made after the violins of Rigart Rubus of St. Petersburg, with flat arching and bevelled edging. Then there was the "Amati Model – fingerboard with inlaid frets and pearl position dots. ... An ideal instrument for students learning without a teacher."

The effort to satisfy every possible demand of their customers continued to be as an important element in the Williamses' programme, as it had been in the first days of the business. Such quality service required a steady increase in the number and variety of instruments offered for sale. The scope of the business at this time is shown by the fact that the total number of employees was about 250, and the payroll of the Oshawa plant alone was over $60,000 annually.

Some of the last photographs of R.S. Williams, showed him in his greenhouse engaged in reading, by then his favourite occupation, and being asked by his son for an opinion on a violin.

The next year the old man died. "Richard Sugden Williams, who passed away at his late residence, "Oaklawn", corner Sherbourne and Wellesley Street, Toronto, Feb. 24, 1906, was one of the city's best known business men and highly esteemed citizens. ... His later years were spent in contributing to the happiness of others and lending a helping hand to many who were in need. Mr. Williams was an exemplary citizen in every walk of life, and in his death Canada lost a pioneer manufacturer of musical instruments; Toronto one of her successful businessmen, the Church a consistent member and liberal supporter, and his family a devoted husband and father."[138]

The contributions of Williams to the development and popularization of music in Canada were aptly characterized in this modest eulogy. However, it should be added that, in the death of R.S. Williams, Canada lost a pioneer connoisseur and collector of musical instruments.

8

R.S. WILLIAMS JR., AS COLLECTOR (1906-1915)

Unique catalogues of rare violins and old musical instruments; the new president as collector and violin expert.

After the death of his father in 1906, Richard Sugden Williams Jr., became the president of the R.S. Williams & Sons Co. Limited in Toronto. The catalogue of the Williams' old violin collection had been issued early that same year, before the death of the former president. The design of the catalogue reflects the firm's reputation for dealing in fine and valuable instruments: a pamphlet tied with a silken cord, its covers are black with gold print; on its cover is a gold seal with the words "Williams Toronto," a wreath, and a violin. The long tradition of the firm and the respected position of the founder are promoted in the catalogue. A portrait of the elder R.S. Williams with a violin is captioned, "The above is a late portrait of our President, R.S. Williams, who is recognized as the father of the violin trade in Canada." Over the portrait is this text: "Established 1849 at Ye Sign of the Big Fiddle." (The year of the establishment of the firm is erratically reported in all documentary materials.)

Frontispiece of the Catalogue of "Williams' Old Violins," 1906. Courtesy Remenyi House of Music, Toronto, Ontario.

The frontispiece has a drawing of a violinist standing in front of a music stand; in his left hand is a violin, in his right a tuning fork. This illustration became common in the firm's publications, and was used on the R.S. Williams Ex Libris. To the upper left and lower right is the motto introduced by Richard Sugden Williams Jr.: "The Key Note of Our Success – Musical Instruments of Quality." This claim is not idle self-promotion, but expresses the general opinion of Williams instruments: " 'Williams Quality' in violins and cellos is a standard appreciated in the most exclusive musical circles."[139]

The pages of the catalogue are embellished with portraits of sixteen famous violinists in small roundels. Under the portrait of Henri Wieniawski (1835-1880), Polish violin virtuoso, composer, and teacher, is this epigraph:

"To perfect that wonder of travel – the locomotive – has perhaps not required the expenditure of more mental strength and application, than to

Repurchase Certificate from the Catalogue of "Williams' Old Violins." Courtesy Remenyi House of Music, Toronto, Ontario.

perfect that wonder of music – the violin."[140]

The preface follows the epigraph, giving advice to the purchaser from the firm's old violin department:

"In purchasing a violin it is well to remember that the ideal tone can only be found in Genuine Old Violins and when purchasing an instrument from our collection you are making an investment that will repay you, not only in satisfaction to yourself, but in a financial way as well. Old violins are steadily advancing in price, and as the supply (unlike other commodities) is limited, we cannot too strongly advise intending purchasers to secure their instruments at once."[141]

The catalogue stipulates the seven "articles" or conditions of purchase. Article four reads, "Old Violins or Cellos will be accepted as part payment and full value allowed when better instruments are purchased." This indicates that R.S. Williams Jr., followed his father's practice in collecting instruments of the violin family, considering trade one of the most effective means of discovering and acquiring fine instruments.[142] The seventh article is a firm assurance of authenticity to the purchaser. "We give a certificate of genuineness with each instrument, signed by our violin expert." No such document has yet been discovered. Perhaps it was similar in form to the Repurchase Certificate, which was given to the buyer on his request, as stated in article six of the conditions.

The catalogue offers old violins, cellos, and bows with a special note to the potential buyer: "The following is a list of the Old Violins now in stock, as this list is continually changing we advise when ordering to name a first, second and third choice."[143] The list contains fifty-two violins, one viola, and two violoncellos of a variety of schools and countries of origin. There is no discernible pattern to the system of numbering: the first violin listed on page 6 is No. 711, while the third violin on page 8 has the catalogue number 9203.

No. 711 is a Franesco Ruggeri (sic) violin "in the highest state of preservation"[144] for $4,000. Next is a Giovan Grancino numbered 710; its price is $3,000.[145] Other instruments in the catalogue are ascribed to Andrea Postachini, Richard Duke, George Craske, Johannes Udalricus Eberle of Prague, Nicholas Didier of Mirecourt, Anton Jais of Mittenwald, Joseph Klotz, Lambert, and Denis. A viola by François Chanot is shown,[146] and a Franceso Ruger (sic) violoncello is reproduced and listed at a price of $1,500.[147]

Bows made by Williams, Johann Glass, and W.E. Hill & Sons, London, are offered, although the advertisement promises a much larger choice: "In this department we carry a very large assortment of bows by all the best modern makers, such as Hill, Tubbs, Bernardel, Vigneron, Albert, Nurnburger, Weichold, ranging in price from $12.00 to $50.00."[148]

Of significant documentary value are a photograph of R.S. Williams Jr., in a "View of our old violin department and library," and a reproduction described as "An old Paganini Concert programme in the Williams Collection."[149] These items are the first published material from the R.S. Williams Collection of old musical instruments and other objects, aside from the three rare old violins published in catalogue No. 31 in 1905. The photograph, taken in the firm's library, shows

"View of our Old Violin Department and Library," with R.S. Williams reading, in the Catalogue of "Williams' Old Violins," page 9. Reproduced from the original photograph. Courtesy Mrs. I.W. Brock, b. Williams, Toronto, Ontario.

numerous valuable specimens in a vault like case and in individual cases. On the wall hangs a violoncello flanked by three instruments, two of which can be recognized as the viola by François Chanot and the violin ascribed to a "Scottish self-educated maker in the 19th century";[150] both instruments are now in the R.S. Williams Collection in the Royal Ontario Museum.

The second catalogue of rare old violins, issued probably a year or two later in 1907 or 1908, shows improvements in the arrangement of the material. Significantly, the pictorial representation of old instruments includes some items that were not for sale, making the publication a collection catalogue as well as a sales catalogue. Repeated from the 1906 catalogue are instructions on "How you can buy," and the photograph of R.S. Williams, Sr., with the violin, accompanied here by this caption: "The above is an excellent likeness of our Late President, Mr. R.S. Williams, the founder of the R.S. Williams & Sons Co. Mr. Williams was also an authority on old violins of international fame."

On the next page is a portrait of R.S. Williams Jr. The catalogue entries follow, arranged by schools. The Italian school is first, and includes the representative makers from the previous catalogue. To the illustrations are added violins ascribed to Giovanni Battista Cerute (*sic*) and Pietro Gurneri (*sic*). (Errors in spelling of foreign names continue in this catalogue.) The French school is represented by violins attributed to J.B. Vuillaume, N. Didier, J.N. Lambert, Nicolas Augustin Chappuy, H. Derazey, and others. A Vuillaume violin and a viola by François Chanot appear on the same page.

The Paganini concert programme reproduction is repeated in this catalogue with the extended caption, "We also have on view in our Old Violin Department a beautiful portrait of Nicola (*sic*) Paganini, date 1831; Also a very interesting letter signed by Paganini." While the programme and the portrait were not included in the collection donated to the Royal Ontario Museum, a letter in French, signed by Paganini, is among the autographs and documents donated by R.S. Williams in 1934.

The most fascinating thing in this second catalogue is the remarkable number of old instruments it contains, of which most were later donated to the ROM. Their pictures are scattered through the catalogue's pages. After the entry for the single representative of the Dutch school, a violin offered as made by "Kleymans of Amsterdam, about 1720"[151] (Cornelius Kleymans worked in Amsterdam from 1670 to 1699), are pictures of three chitarrone lutes. These typical Baroque instruments now represent that period very well in the Royal Ontario Museum's collection of musical instruments. Study of these rare instruments, however, has changed some of the collector's attributions, particularly the dates. When bass lutes were developed they had long necks with additional peg-boxes, and were strung with long bass strings. The archlutes are represented in the R.S. Williams Collection by a Theorbo and three Chitarrones. The alteration of stringing and the appearance of the archlute interfered with the preservation of old lutes, because during the second half of the seventeenth century, old lutes were rebuilt as archlutes. The Chitarrones and the Theorbo from the Williams collection could be earlier

74

instruments altered in this way; the names on their labels are so far unknown.

Many violins of the English school are offered for sale, including instruments attributed to well-known makers such as Richard Duke, Daniel Parker, John Betts of London, Matthew Hardy and Son of Edinburgh, Thomas Perry of Dublin, Benjamin Banks of Salisbury, and George Craske of Manchester. Some of the instruments are introduced simply as "Old English Violins" of unknown masters; some of them have the important note, "From the Collection of Hart and Son, London."[152]

Instead of illustrations of the English violins, this section shows pictures of other old instruments and objects in the collection. Included are instruments that are identical with those now in the Royal Ontario Museum: the Rauch viola d'amore of 1757, and the small tenor viol made by Johann Joseph Elsler in 1746.[153] The musical objects were such things as an old Italian violin case from about 1700 (also given to the Museum).

Among the more unusual instruments shown in the catalogue are two kits or pocket violins. These peculiar instruments, some English, some French, and some Italian, were used by dancing masters and itinerant entertainers of the seventeenth and eighteenth centuries. Also illustrated are a Pandora, and Italian kind of bass cittern, and a Chitarra Battente,[154] a wire-strung guitar played with a plectrum and widely used in Italy in the seventeenth and eighteenth centuries. For some reason, the instruments in the catalogue representing the viola d'amore collection were not given to the Museum. The instruments were described as a "Viola d'Amore, 19th century. P. Mangenot, Mirecourt, France," and a "Viola d'Amore, 19th century. (German), maker unknown."[155] But only two of the four citterns later given to the Museum appear in this catalogue.[156] Although the cittern had only a small place in serious music, it was much enjoyed by the public. Under the name "English Guitar" the new cittern became so popular that after 1750 it was the fashionable musical instrument for lady amateurs. Some examples show how handsomely the instruments were made to fit with the furnishings of the period. The instrument described as a German Cither has been identified as a Waldzither of the late eighteenth century.

The next section of the catalogue concentrates on new merchandise offered for sale. The violins of the German school are ascribed to makers such as Jacob Weiss and Johann Georg Voight. There is a list headed "Special list of Genuine Old Violins of the German School, the makers names are unknown to us." Subsequent pages advertise accessories to the instruments: "Art Violin bows" were made by W.E. Hill & Sons, London, by Johann Glass, Leipzig, and by E. Sartory, Paris; two pages offer violin cases, violin strings, and fittings.

The three R.S. Williams Collection catalogues of instruments are the only ones of their kind in Canada; the last probably dates from 1910. We cannot be sure of the year of publication, as even the printing company's name on the back of the cover was left without a date, and reads, "Press of the 5" x 1" Letter-Envelope Company, Ltd., Toronto." A hint at the date is given in a letter on the last page, on which Williams' Italian violin strings are advertised. The caption and the text of the letter read as follows:

"Read what Herr Ondricek, the great teacher of Kubelik and formerly of the Kneisel Quartette, says about the Williams Italian Strings: New York, Oct. 24th, 1910. My dear Williams, I have been using your Italian Strings for the past five years, and have found them to be the best in the world. Kindly duplicate my last order. Yours very truly, K. Ondricek."[157]

A second indication of the date of publication is the inclusion in the discussion of the Italian school of two Amati violins that were not mentioned in the previous catalogues. The acquisition of these violins by R.S. Williams is revealed in a *Toronto World* article May 1, 1910:

"Last season, through Mr. Williams' European connections, he was lucky enough to secure two of the finest Nicholas Amati violins. One of these is now in the possession of Mr. John S. Loudon, Assistant General Manager of the Standard Bank; the other is still in the possession of Mr. Williams."[158]

The design of this third catalogue is different again. It has no illustrations except for the portrait medallions of famous violinists, one at each corner of the page. With minor changes the contents of the entries for various schools remains the same. This last catalogue also includes a section on violas, violoncellos and "Rare Old violin bows," also divided according to schools. However, the inclusion of a Canadian school of violin makers is a pleasant surprise, as it recognizes that the violin was playing a significant role in the cultivation and preservation of the love of music in Canada.

Violin making in Canada is not an old tradition. It begins only with the Lyonnais family of Quebec in the 1820s. Then Augustin Lavallée (1816-1903) became known as a violin maker in St. Hyacinthe; with his helpers he built more than one hundred violins. The entries of the Canadian school appear on the same page of the catalogue that offers violins of the Dutch and Spanish schools. The Canadian makers are William Godley of Lunenburg, Nova Scotia, and William Adams, Joseph Hugil, and John Fortong of Toronto.[159]

If these catalogues are somewhat perplexing to the critical reader, they nevertheless represent a first organized attempt, through collecting and trade, to secure the best for contemporary and future violinists in the young but developing life of music in Canada. In this endeavour, too, it was the instinct and natural talent of R.S. Williams Jr., his feel for tradition and his years of experience with musical instruments, rather than any formal education, that gave him the ability to discover and select for his collection instruments of the highest quality. The task was more difficult than in the days of the first known connoisseur and collector of old Italian violins, Luigi Tarisio (d. 1854). Tarisio had the advantage of usually finding an instrument in its original condition, so that he could study its characteristics without fear of confusion. Williams and his contemporaries, on the other hand, had to deal with the increasingly common practice of removing labels with unmarketable names and substituting, in fact counterfeiting, the labels of well-known makers.

The rather laudatory article on R.S. Williams Jr., in the Sunday issue of *Toronto World* of May 1, 1910, appears to have been prompted by the publication of this last catalogue. The article was written by the Musical Editor under the title, "Canadian Has World-Wide Reputation as Violin Expert," with the subtitle, "A sketch of R.S. Williams with notes about his work and treasures in old violins and violin bows." This public recognition of Williams' achievement as a collector reveals a great deal about his personal attitude to collecting.

"Mr. Williams is a familiar figure on the streets of Toronto, and an ardent supporter of classical music in the city. ... He is the acknowledged violin expert of Canada, his specialty being the authoritative discovery and distribution of the finest old violins. In this matter his education began very early under his father...who was also a violin expert."[160]

The article, after mentioning his education and experience, concludes: "R.S. Williams...has learned all that the European connoisseurs know, and has added to his store of knowledge from his own observations and talks with the virtuosi violinists of the European Continent."[161] Although the writer has perhaps tended to exaggerate, there is other evidence to support his statements about the sources of Williams' knowledge and experience.

The reputation of R.S. Williams Jr., as an expert on violins and a collector of valuable instruments had spread among musicians as well.

"Mischa Elman, the brilliant young violinist, who for two seasons has been soloist with the Toronto Symphony Orchestra, heard of Mr. Williams' reputation as an authoritative expert in old violins and violin bows, and learned that he had in his possession two beautifully toned Nicolas Amatis (treasures of the violin world) and also an exceedingly precious Vuillaume bow, valued at $200,000. When Mr. Elman arrived in Toronto for his second concert as soloist with the Toronto Symphony Orchestra at Massey Hall, the first thing he did was to seek out the only Canadian expert in old violins and violin bows, and after spending a few days with Mr. R.S. Williams the latter with his customary generosity, presented to Mischa Elman the Vuillaume bow, which, as Elman said, at the time of presentation, he regarded as the most valuable in existence."[162]

The acquisition of the Amati violins seemed to be some sort of sign that Williams had become an important figure in the music world:

"This, and the further fact that Mr. Williams was fortunate enough to secure this season the celebrated string bass, made by Gasparo da Salo, one of the famous Brescian makers, caused the publishers of Music Trades in New York to recognize Mr. Williams as one of the greatest living experts in old violins, and to ask him to contribute, as he

Mischa Elman, his sister and father visiting R.S. Williams' headquarters, c. 1920. Courtesy Mrs. I.W. Brock, b. Williams, Toronto, Ontario.

did, a full page illustrated article to this journal on the subject."[163]

This double bass has been in the Royal Ontario Museum since 1915 when R.S. Williams Jr., added it to the collection that he gave in 1913. It is attributed to Gasparo Bertolotti da Salo, the famous violin maker who was born in Salo in 1540 and died in Brescia in 1609, and it is dated about 1600. It was in the collection of the celebrated double bass soloist Domenico Dragonetti (1763-1846), who presented it to the Duke of Leinster, after whose death it was sold by the Duke's nephew to William E. Hill & Sons. In 1909 it was acquired by R.S. Williams.

In the same issue and section of the *Toronto World* are articles described as "Specially contributed to the *Sunday World* by R.S. Williams – British Makers of Violins and on Violin Tone." It is obvious that Williams was distinguishing himself as a Canadian who was gaining a name internationally, mostly through his knowledge of violins:

"R.S. Williams has now dispersed

all examples of the fine "King of Instruments" in Canada, and a considerable number of those in the United States have found their way there from the Williams' collection, and some have even gone back to Europe from the same collection. It is a credit to Canada that this land has a native born son who is recognized the world over as one of the absolutely first-rate experts in judging the dates, and in telling the history and quality of old violins."[164]

Although R.S. Williams Jr., was kept busy with many responsibilities for his expanding business, he never lost his love of collecting. In addition to the assortment of violins, his collection contained a remarkable number of other musical instruments, autograph letters, and documents of famous musicians, singers, composers, and other personalities of the world of music. Also included were small but valuable collections of rare music sheets, scores, and books, as well as paintings, prints, and sculpted works relating to music.

A correspondence that lasted from 1911 until 1921 between R.S. Williams Jr., and Otokar Ševčik (1852-1934), the noted Czech violinist and violin teacher, shows that Williams was the patron of a young Canadian violinist named Louis Rottenberg. Williams apparently paid Rottenberg's expenses while he studied under Ševčik, in Prague and at his summer country residence in the town of Prachatice near Pisek. Nothing is heard of this protégé after 1921, when he was mentioned in the *Prager Tagblatt*. Ševčik sent the clipping to a Mr. Loudon in Toronto. It can be assumed that he is the same J.S. Loudon who purchased one of the two Amatis from R.S. Williams. There is no clue as to how London and Williams were related to Ševčik's pupil.[165]

The significance of the Williams /Ševčik correspondence is manifold. While identifying R.S. Williams Jr., as a supporter of young Canadian talent, it is also a further proof of his personal contacts in the world of music: not only with violin makers, collectors, and connoisseurs, but also with such a renowned violinist as Ševčik, who taught such famous violinists as Jan Kubelik and Marie Hall. If this great violin teacher had not respected Williams' reputation in the violin world, he would hardly have accepted Rottenberg as a student with insufficient musical preparedness (as he complained in one of his letters to Williams).[166] In 1904 Harriette von Kunits accompanied her husband, violinist Luigi von Kunits (1870-1932), on a visit to Professor Ševčik, and wrote, "Ševčik had turned away hundreds of applicants."[167]

In Ševčik's letter of November 13, 1911, the maestro thanks Williams for an "India Rubber Chin Rest" and praises the product, as it was not so heavy as others and was comfortable to hold. An article in the *Canadian Music Trade Journal* explains this reference to a violin chin rest, under the title "R.S. Williams commences manufacture of violin rest invented by him":

"The sore chin, so frequently a complaint of violinists, gave Mr. Williams the idea of a soft rest, and his invention, as now on the market, is the result. He had a number of rests made up of soft India rubber and gave them to a few violinist

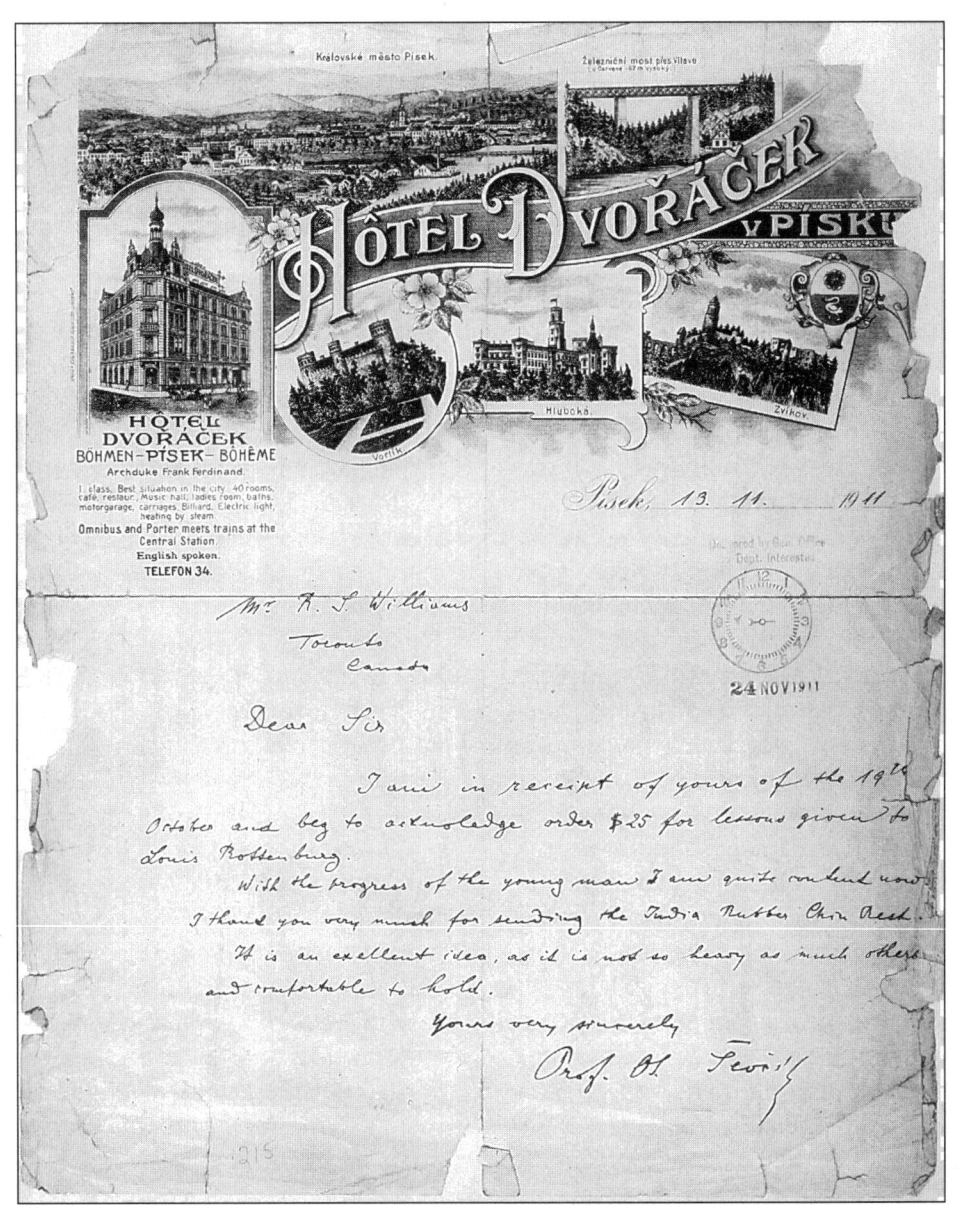

Ševčík's letter to R.S. Williams, of November 13, 1911. In the R.O.M. Collections.

friends to test them. After three years' trial the results were so pleasing that Mr. Williams decided to put them on the market in Canada and the United States."[168]

In the list of fifteen leading violinists who congratulated Williams and endorsed the invention were Ševčik and Luigi von Kunits. Professor Ševčik was among the first experts to whom the chin rest was sent for trial. The same *Canadian Music Trade Journal* article continues with this description:

"[It] required but slight pressure of the chin to hold the violin in position: is soft and flexible, will not chafe the most delicate skin. Much lighter in weight than many chin rests now on the market. The metal bars are much farther apart than most chin rests, thereby distributing the pressure on the ribs of the violin, thus avoiding the chances of cracking or damaging the instrument. The top of the chin rest is easily detached and can be replaced at a nominal figure. Not so rigid as the old style rests, thus allowing freedom of motion. Sets well up from the violin, thus avoiding the use of pad in most cases."[169]

Ševčik's correspondence ends suddenly with a letter to London in Toronto. Unfortunately no letter written by Williams or Loudon to Ševčik is known.

The correspondence of R.S. Williams Jr., with the members of the Hill family of London, reveals a relationship that was long-lasting and of more than a business nature. Since 1905, fine quality bows made by the Hills had been advertised in the Williams catalogues. *The Williams Old Violin Collection* offers an "Old English violin – about 1760," said to have been recently repaired by Messrs. Hill & Son, of London, England; its price was $200.[170] Williams' cooperation with the Hills suggests that the renowned English family of violin experts was an influence on his attitude and growth as a collector. His journeys to Germany and France resulted in close business relations with other manufacturers mentioned in the 1910 catalogue. To them should be added Eugene Sartory of Paris, whose bows were admired throughout the world.

The years immediately following the death of his father saw R.S. Williams Jr., come into his own as a collector of rare instruments. This is amply illustrated by the catalogue of his firm as well as by other contemporary sources. The same article that announced his chin-rest innovation also acknowledged Williams' position as a collector: "That violin collecting is his hobby is well known. His collection includes rare specimens of almost unbelievable value."[171]

9

A GREAT GIFT TO TORONTO AND CANADA (1902-1916)

The New Scale Williams Piano; the opening of the Williams Music House; the donation of the collection to the Royal Ontario Museum.

After the reorganization of the Williams' business enterprise in 1902, the Williams Piano Company proceeded to achieve a new level of success. Although the company ceased to be under the direct control of the Williams family after the retirement of Robert Williams as president in 1903, his successors were experts in piano building. They initiated an entire revision in scale, acoustics, tone, touch, action, and case design that resulted in the introduction of the "New Scale Williams Piano." (One of the first of these, as mentioned in chapter seven, was presented to R.S. Williams, Sr., in 1904.) This improved instrument increased sales, and the output of the piano works increased from two or three instruments a day to a total of some three thousand a year, including the popular player pianos, which became part of the manufacturing programme in 1906.

The success of the new firm was a credit to its leaders. The president and managing director was Frederick Bull, who in 1906 had joined the Williams Piano Company as vice-president and manager, and who bought out Robert Williams in 1907; vice-president and manager for Eastern Canada was George E. Dies in Montreal; and the Western manager was E.C. Scythes in Winnipeg. Under the new management, the foremost workers of the original Williams company stayed on: for example, George Burt, the first superintendent under Robert Williams; John Newton, who had joined the factory on its establishment in 1889; James O'Connor, one of the first employees; and many others from the best of the "old piano men."[172]

At the Canadian National Exhibition in 1913 the Williams Piano Company exhibited its New Scale Pianos. The exhibit proved to be a powerful advertisement for the company. Also useful in this regard was the fact that, as a contemporary report stated, "Mme. Melba, who commences her concert season this month with a tour of Canada, has selected the New Scale Williams piano, and

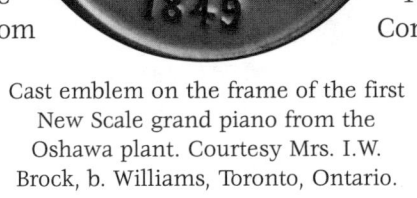

Cast emblem on the frame of the first New Scale grand piano from the Oshawa plant. Courtesy Mrs. I.W. Brock, b. Williams, Toronto, Ontario.

Action finishing of the Oshawa factory, c. 1914. Courtesy Mr. Th. Bouckley, Oshawa, Ontario.

Teresa Careno will also use this make exclusively."[173] The inclusion of the improved player pianos called "Meister Touch" in the class of the New Scale Williams indicates that the term "New Scale Williams" covered a number of improved instruments, including the New Scale Williams cabinet pianos made for Ennis & Co., Hamilton. Ennis later became a brand name of the Williams Piano Company.

The success of the new products caught the attention of the Toronto Symphony Orchestra, which used the New Scale Williams piano in performances in Massey Hall. The Toronto Symphony Orchestra was formed by Frank S. Welsman in 1906, the year the founder of the Williams musical-instrument manufacturing business died, as the Toronto Conservatory Symphony Orchestra; after two years it changed its name to Toronto Symphony Orchestra and acquired semiprofessional status. The two firms, R.S. Williams & Sons Co. and the Williams Piano Company, were on the lists of sponsors of the orchestra, along with other leading firms in the musical-instrument industry and music publishing business of Toronto.

Six years into the presidency of R.S. Williams Jr., in R.S. Williams & Sons Co., one of the greatest projects of the firm came into completion. In 1912 the new Williams business "palace" was erected at 145 Yonge Street. The impact its con-

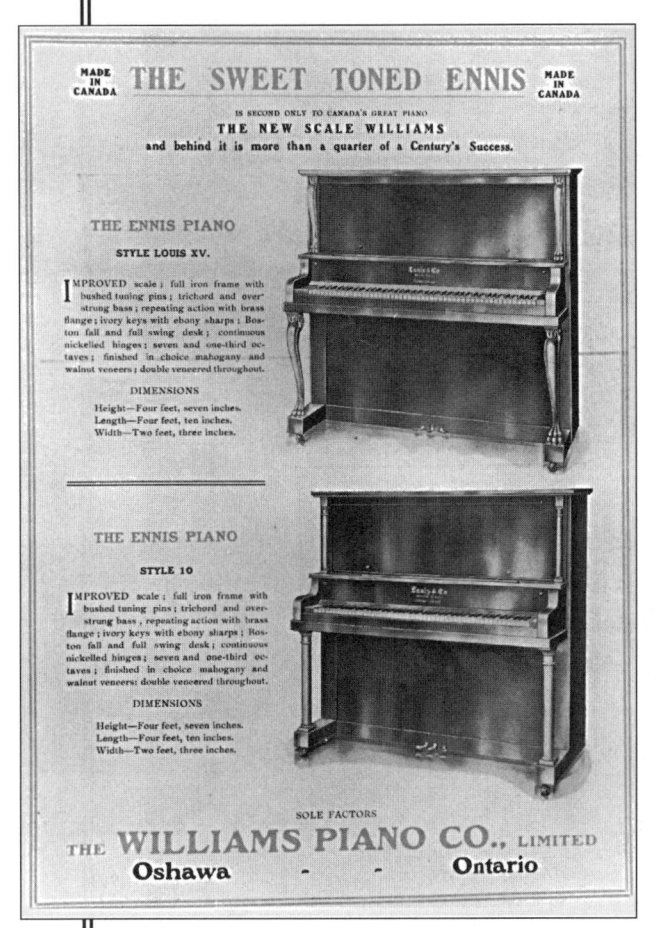

The "Ennis Piano" from the Williams Piano Co. from advertisement, 1912. Courtesy National Library of Canada, Music Division, Ottawa, Ontario.

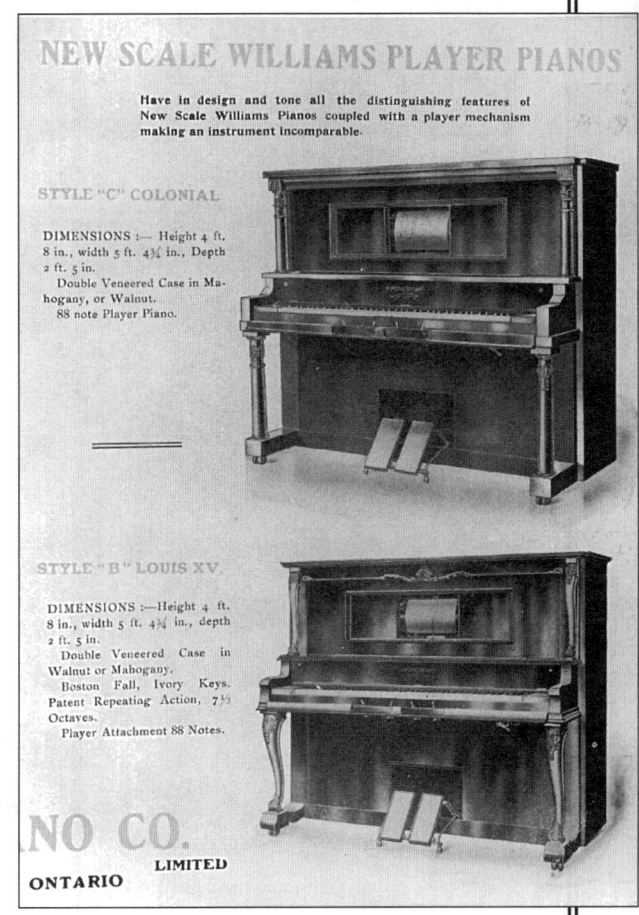

New Scale Williams player piano from advertisement, 1912. Courtesy National Library of Canada, Music Division, Ottawa, Ontario.

struction had at the time is understandable:

"Toronto is a city of but few reinforced concrete buildings, and of the few there are only two which reach a height of ten stories. The most modern of these is the R.S. Williams Building, on the east side of Yonge Street, between Adelaide and Richmond streets, just now being completed.

This building has a frontage on Yonge Street of twenty-three feet six inches and is one hundred feet deep. The street elevation is treated architecturally as one large panel with a glass front to each floor. The concrete on the front of the building up the sides is faced with glazed terra cotta."[174]

The emblem on the building, for so long the Big Fiddle, was now a lyre and other musical instruments, with the initials "R S W" in concrete. The organization of the merchandise in the fabulous new music store was illustrated on the facade of the building. First and foremost the new building was a monument to the late R.S. Williams, Sr., who in 1856 had started the little musical-instrument business that achieved such development. At the time of the opening of the new building, the company had branches in Montreal, Winnipeg and Calgary.

The new building was planned with an eye to the provision of special services and to greater efficiency. Innovative ideas in design were sought by members of the firm on their many visits to modern buildings in the United States. The building was completed on schedule, and was described as absolutely fireproof; even the window frames, floors, interior trim, and partitions were of non-flammable materials.

When R.S. Williams & Sons Co. settled into the magnificent building at 145 Yonge Street, the stock included almost every musical instrument imaginable and everything pertaining to the music business."A special room on the ground floor has been constructed for the old violin department, on which Mr. R.S. Williams lavishes much attention. He has one of the most valuable of the world's collections, containing instruments that are the envy of musicians in the largest centres on this continent and in Europe. Rare specimens are being added as they can be secured. A special fireproof vault joins this department, for the safe storage of the costly instruments. The firm's museum includes a collection of antique instruments, many secured at great cost, and only after long and patient research. This department is being constantly visited by the general public, and musicians who appreciate the educative value of such a collection. The music library in connection includes many valuable and rare books."[175]

This is the first clear indication that the R.S. Williams Collection was being presented as an educational unit, deservedly called a special museum.

The report of the formal opening of the Williams "Music House" provides a picture of the environment in which the collection was displayed, the extent of the Williams enterprise, and some of the people responsible for it.[176] According to that report, on January 21 and 22, 1913, Torontonians by the thousands visited the new ten-storey building. The public was invited through "prominent and well-worded advertising in the daily newspapers," and four thousand invitations were sent to individuals and institutions. The festivities included musical programmes performed on four different floors.

An electric elevator whisked the

The new R.S. Williams House, 145 Yonge, as published in the *Canadian Music and Trade Journal* in August, 1912. Courtesy National Library of Canada, Music Division, Ottawa, Ontario.

visitors to the tenth floor, where the general offices, the advertising department, and the offices of the general manager and cashier were located. The visitors then walked downstairs and were met at each floor by someone to show them around. On the ninth floor were samples of the wholesale merchandise, under the charge of F. Shelton. A Mr. White gave demonstrations of the Wurlitzer electric orchestras that were finding an important market in the moving picture theatres. On the eighth and seventh floors was the wholesale stock of the Edison talking machine under the charge of G.B. Petch, while on the sixth floor J.J. Dinsmore was in charge of wholesale small goods. The repair department was located at the rear of the fifth floor, while the perforated rolls for player pianos were kept in the front part.

The piano department occupied the fourth and third floors. A series of recitals by members of the Toronto Symphony Orchestra was given on the fourth floor. On the third floor, several connecting soundproof demonstration rooms led off the main corridor. Visitors alighting from the elevator at this floor stepped into a large display salon, where in the intermission of a piano recital people listened to a player piano demonstration.

"On this floor is the museum, being a unique and exceedingly valuable collection of rare instruments, many without a duplicate. This proved to be a continual attraction, and some visitors spent hours in examining objects of curiosity. To this museum R.S. Williams & Sons Co. invited the general public at all times."[177]

Sound-reproducing machines were displayed on the second floor, among them various types of Victrolas and the new Edison disc phonograph which many of the visitors were seeing for the first time. Jeffrey Ford, manager of this department, and his salesmen were busy giving demonstrations to the visitors in ten soundproof rooms.

On the ground floor was located the retail stock of small goods, The old violin department occupied a specially equipped space in the rear.

"This was a particularly attractive room to violin connoisseurs, who could appreciate the value of the instruments shown and the painstaking labour involved to secure them. This is the particular department of the firm's President, Mr. R.S. Williams, who personally mingled with the visitors, showing them around, and helping them to feel welcome."[178]

The report goes on to name the leading officers of R.S. Williams and Sons Co. at the time of the opening: the general manager, H.G. Stanton, who personally met many of the firm's patrons on the main floor; John A. Croden, the assistant general manager, who had recently joined the Toronto staff; and Thomas Birdsall, manager of the piano department, who looked after all visitors to the piano showrooms. C.R. Coleman, manager of the Montreal branch, was present at the opening, and Arthur Mandy and H.D. Cockburn, both "road men," had returned to headquarters to assist in looking after visitors. The firm's cashier, William Middleton, just a week before the official opening of the new

Williams building, had celebrated his eighty-first birthday; 1913 marked his thirty-seventh year with the Williams establishment. B.A. Trestrail, the firm's advertising manager, handed to the visitors on their way out a souvenir and a card thanking them for their visit.

This was the first time an article in the press had presented the names of the firm's organizers, those responsible for the achievements of the company under the presidency of R.S. Williams Jr. The people involved in management, such as Middleton, were almost all of the old school, and had joined the firm under the late founder. For example, Stanton, who was for ten years the firm's general manager, commenced his career with the Williams firm in 1890; he had been engaged by the branch in London, Ontario, then under the management of John A. Croden. Stanton served sixteen years under the presidency of R.S. Williams, Sr.; under the founder's guidance he was chosen for the important position of general manager in 1903, at the time the old president was gradually withdrawing from active involvement in the business. In August 1913, eight months after the opening of the Williams building, Stanton was elected vice-president of the company at a meeting of the shareholders.[179]

On June 12, 1913, the sixth Annual Cavort of R.S. Williams & Sons Co. was held. It was a successful holiday for staff, officers, and guests. More than 150 people attended the merry outing, crossing the lake on the steamer *Chippewa*, and spending the day at Victoria Park, Niagara Falls. The Hamilton branch staff travelled to the outing by Grand Trunk Railway, making this a record-sized outing of the house. It was noted that "Mr.

R. S. Williams Executives of Long Service With the House

H. G. STANTON, Vice-president and general manager—38 years.

A. M. KINCADE, Director, over 28 years.

WILLIAM MIDDLETON, Secretary, over 50 years.

R.S. Williams Executives of long service with the house. Captions from the *Canadian Music Trades Journal*, No. 4., 1924. Courtesy National Library of Canada, Music Division, Ottawa, Ontario.

Williams enjoyed himself as much as any youngster, and in the ball game looked after first base in his usual style," but the report expressed regret at the absence of H.G. Stanton, who was on his annual visit to the branches in Winnipeg and Calgary.[180] The oldest participant, in terms of service, was John Brown, who had been the firm's piano mover for thirty-one years, having started work with the firm R.S. Williams and Son.

In September of the year in which the new building was opened, Richard Sugden, Jr., and his wife Alma celebrated the birth of their fourth child and first boy. The baby was christened Richard Sugden Williams III, and was later called Dick.

The year 1913 also turned out to be extraordinary for Williams' collecting activities. In the new building the fine collection amassed by Williams and his late father was presented as a small, special museum of musical instruments and music. This year saw this unusual achievement, unique in Canada, moved beyond the context of the family firm, and donated to the Royal Ontario Museum of Archaeology.

> "The valuable collection of antique musical instruments, manuscripts and books that have comprised so interesting a museum at the sales rooms of R.S. Williams & Sons Co. Ltd., Toronto, and which are the personal property of Mr. R.S. Williams, head of the firm, have been loaned to the Royal Ontario Museum of Archaeology, located on Bloor Street, Toronto. Mr. Williams' collection is one of great value, and his generosity in thus placing it should be greatly appreciated by the general public."[181]

Williams' reason for transferring his collection was to secure its expert maintenance and full utilization in the most suitable institution in the city of Toronto, which the Royal Ontario Museum undoubtedly was. Additional motives, however, are suggested in the recollection of violin maker George Heinl. Through R.S. Williams' connection with the firm of W.E. Hill & Sons in London, Heinl had been transferred around 1912 from England to the Williams' violin repair workshop as a highly skilled expert of the Austrian school. Heinl remembered the special vault that housed the collection of rare old violins, and recalled that the store manager (probably the general manager, H.G. Stanton) disapproved of storing the collection at the business location when the company needed extra sales space. The president apparently complied by selling some very valuable violins to make room. Heinl also knew, however, that R.S. Williams' antique collection was not for sale.[182]

The R.S. Williams Collection, one of the first major gifts to the Royal Ontario Museum, was received just one year after the museum opened in 1912. Of the correspondence between the donor and Dr. C.T. Currelly, first director of the Royal Ontario Museum of Archaeology, a letter from Dr. Currelly is the earliest preserved document:

To the R.S. Williams Co.

Sirs,
Re the presentation of the R.S. Williams Collection of Musical Instruments to the Royal Ontario

Museum of Archaeology. In response to your request for a statement of conditions under which the Museum receives exhibits, I beg to state that when an article or articles are presented to the Museum that the Museum cases, exhibits and guards to the best of its ability such exhibits. The donor is free to choose what name shall appear on the labels and his wishes are met in every way that does not tend to injure the general unity of the Museum. ... In this way the donor is free from all expenses whatever and the Museum does its best to show its gratitude for all objects that are secured. As soon as possible collections will be published in order that their usefulness may reach beyond the boundaries of those who may see them. Please let me take this opportunity of thanking you most heartily both officially and privately for giving the people of this country a collection which will be of such great interest.

Yours very truly
C.T. Currelly[183]

A letter of August 6, 1913 gives a hint of how difficult it was for R.S. Williams to part with his collection, and of his desire to use every opportunity to be actively involved with it.

"Enclosed please find list of antiques delivered to you recently. I still have other specimens which I would like to see you personally about before delivering them.

In regard to the arranging and labelling of this collection, please do not fail to call of my [sic] for any assistance you may need."[184]

It is possible that moving the collection of old musical instruments out of the new Williams building was actually beneficial to the business. At least there was no need to produce bulky publications such as the special catalogues of 1906, 1908, and 1910. However, having moved the museum did not prevent R.S. Williams Jr., from continuing to demonstrate his deep interest and ambition both in collecting rare musical instruments and in supporting the violin trade of the firm. Through his connoisseurship and personal contacts he continued his attempts to provide the best merchandise and the best violin repair and maintenance services.

In the Preface to his *Catalogue of Rare and Modern Books on the History of Music*, Williams describes one such business transaction that probably predates the donation to the Museum:

"I also have a catalogue of the works of Job Ardern, a quaint Old English maker. Together with Mr. Arthur Hill of London, we purchased all the examples left after his death, half of which we imported into Canada. A good many of these are now bearing imitation Italian labels, a number finding their way into the United States."[185]

Job Ardern was born in 1826, and lived his whole life at Wilmslow in Cheshire. A carpenter by trade, he commenced the hobby of violin making in 1855 and produced over five hundred instruments. He was a craftsman deeply in love with his art, and he made little or no effort to dispose of his violins. At his death in 1912, nearly all of his instruments were acquired by Hill & Sons. After certain examples were given expert finishing touches, they were placed on the market with prices between £10 and £20 ($40-$80). Many were dispatched to Canada.[186]

In 1914 R.S. Williams purchased for J.S. Loudon of Toronto a "fine viola d'amore." This is documented in the article "Renaissance of the viola d'amore" by Britten (a pseudonym) in the *Canadian Journal of Music*. The article mentions Williams' Mangenot copy made perhaps fifty years before, "which has been heard several times in Toronto. It has the typical blindfold head, seven strings, six sympathetic strings and finger pegs for all."[187]

A short article under the title "Violins old and rare" gives more details of Williams' collecting of rare instruments, and indicates that R.S. Williams Jr., expanded the firm's publishing activity:

> "A series of interesting little booklets have been issued by the R.S. Williams & Sons Co., dealing exclusively with the old fiddle department, which is the particular and special business and hobby of the firm's President, Mr. R.S. Williams. ... Among the little booklets referred to, one is devoted exclusively to what is known as the Earl of Aylesford Stradivari of 1683. It is supposed that the Earl of Aylesford secured it from Italy through the celebrated violinist Gardini [sic]. ... Another booklet refers only to bows of ancient origin. To François Turcote [sic], born in 1747, is credited the model of the bow, and which has not been improved upon. He obtained for his best bows, mounted in gold and tortoise, approximately the equivalent of $50 or $60. These now bring over $500."[188]

No one has had the luck to find any of these "little booklets," but the *Canadian Journal of Music* in March 1916 paid special attention to that particular Stradivari violin, with photographs of its front and back on the cover, and an article under the title "Earl of Aylesford Stradivari, A.D. 1683."[189]

The writer of the article is unknown, but it appears in a journal with a certain amount of credibility; the fact that such an authority as Luigi von Kunits was involved in the direction of this monthly journal lends authority to the report.

"The instrument is in remarkable state of preservation and shows the care and reverence that has been bestowed upon it by its late owners. The earliest records we have of this violin date back to the later part of the XVIII century, when it was in possession of the Earl of Aylesford, who, we have every reason to believe, obtained it from Italy through the medium of Gardini [sic], the celebrated violinist, with whom he was acquainted.

Lord Aylesford retained possession of this instrument until 1822, when it passed into the hands of Geo. Ware, Esq., a well-known English violinist of that period. In 1828 it was sold on the recommendation of Dodd, the well-known English violin maker, to a Mr. Hunter, presumably an amateur. Some years later it passed into the hands of another

English violinist, who retained it for many years and at whose death it came into the possession of a relative, from whom it was acquired by well known London dealers, Messrs. W.E. Hill & Sons, from whom it was purchased by Mr. R.S. Williams. Out of respect for the late owner, Mr. Williams does not feel at liberty to divulge the name at present, but after the lapse of some years, should it be desired by the purchaser, he will be only too pleased to make good the omission."

The erratic spelling of the name of the famous Italian violinist in the Williams booklet and in the *Canadian Music Trade Journal* passed also into the article in the *Canadian Journal of Music*; the violinist's name was Felice de Giardini (1716-1796).[190] He is mentioned in a 1902 book by the Hill brothers, *Antonio Stradivari, his life & work*, in connection with the Aylesford bass or violoncello, and in the following entry in a book by William Henley, about Antonio Stradivari:

"1663. The "Earl of Aylesford" Owned by the famous Giardini, who sold it to Earl. Bought by George Ware, English violinist, 1882. Passed into the hands of Hill & Sons. Sent to America. Owned by Lidus von Giltry (virtuoso from Geneva), 1930. Influence of Amati very pronounced in all parts. Now owned by Miss Elizabeth Gloor."[191]

It is regrettable that it has not been possible to confirm more about this instrument and its travels than that it was "sent to America," because it was R.S. Williams Jr., who purchased it and brought it to Toronto. In any event this incident shows Williams' involvement in the highest strata of connoisseurship, collecting and trading rare old violins.[192]

Keeping in the tradition his father started under the sign of the Big Fiddle, R.S. Williams Jr., extended the success of the family business to benefit the community. The generous donation to the public of the fruit of two generations' endeavour enhances the fact that both Williamses were pioneers in collecting and connoisseurship in Canada.

10

THE LAST DECADES OF THE FIRM (1914-1931)

The Edison Phonograph; the war years; the violins of Auguste Delivet; seventy-five years of musical service

The Williams' policy of combining the manufacture and trade of small musical instruments with the production of reed organs and, later, pianos proved to be profitable for the firm financially and for society musically. The wide-ranging, well-balanced stock of R.S. Williams & Sons was a definite business asset.

"The firm (R.S. Williams & Sons Co., Limited) are the only makers of small instruments in Canada, manufacturing any instrument from a jewsharp to a pipe organ."[193]

The role of the pipe organ and of the other large instruments in the Williams business programme is obvious. But such a modest, simple instrument as the jews-harp (also known as the Jaws harp and Jew's harp) also had its place. H.Y. Clayton, at one time sales manager for R.S. Williams & Sons, recalled that he sometimes had difficulty in obtaining delivery from the Customs House of such smaller merchandise. In one instance the firm informed a customs official that the duty had been paid and customs cleared on a case of jews-harps seven months earlier, but that they had never been received. The official said, "Well, this is the first time I ever knew a Jew's harp was a musical instrument."[194]

Its long tradition of stocking a wide variety of small goods prevented the Williams' firm from making the mistake of many retail stores when public demand for the talking machine first developed, and substituting talking machines for pianos. Instead, R.S. Williams Jr., promoted Edison's phonograph as an important means of popularizing music. It can be assumed that he fully agreed with the contemporary opinion in the musical-instrument business that the small-goods department should be run in conjunction with the talking-machine department, not replaced by it. Some people in the trade maintained that the talking machine had become a distinct factor itself in the creation and development of musical taste and that, for example, the greater interest of the public in buying music in sheets and books was the result of the influence of phonograph records and player piano rolls.

How seriously he took this idea can be seen in the organization of Williams' Edison wholesale department. There are even records of his personal contacts with the ingenious inventor. In 1914, Williams visited the Edison plant in Orange, New Jersey, accompanied by B.A. Trestrail, his advertising manager, Glen Petch, manager of the Edison wholesale department, and Jeffrey Ford, manager of the retail phonograph department. They spoke with Edison himself, who explained to them the development of his inventions. In particular they learned that "the synchronization of different voices and different instruments is a feature upon which Mr. Edison made countless experiments, before putting out the present high class Edison disc record."[195] That the firm's attention to the talking-machine business grew in the following years is also documented by rare photographs from the Edison Dealers' Convention which Williams organized in 1917.

The spread of recorded music in Toronto and in the rest of Canada had been very quick as something of a craze for the talking machine developed. Once the trend had begun, many firms other than Edison offered products for sale. Among them was The Disk Talking Machine Co., established in 1903. In 1904 Columbia Records of Canada established a factory for record pressing and graphophone assembly in Toronto. In 1913 the Pathé Records and Pathephones Agency and wholesale business was started; Canadian Vitaphone Company announced their plans to produce records; and Victor Talking Machines also appeared. The Williams Piano Company's new phonograph was introduced at the 1919 Canadian National Exhibition.

Encouraging the popularity of

Members of the Williams' organization and Edison representatives on the lawn of Mrs. R.S. Williams' residence, Toronto, 1917. Courtesy National Library of Canada, Music Division, Ottawa, Ontario.

recorded music could reward the music business in two ways: those who were dealers in phonographic items would benefit from the increased interest in music, as would those who dealt in more traditional musical instruments and merchandise. One very interesting event in the promotion of recorded music in Toronto was the Edison Concert in Massey Hall in 1916. A small article provides the contemporary atmosphere:

> "A concert...in the interest of the "Bantam's Battalion" was of an unusual nature. Four well-known artists contributed the programme, singing in unison. The Edison Diamond Disc was furnished by the R.S. Williams & Sons Co., Ltd., and the faultless synchronizing of the living voices with the reproduced voices was a delightful surprise to the audience."[196]

That Edison considered his invention a tool in musical education is indicated by his gift of a phonograph to the Royal Ontario Museum. A photograph shows a group of children listening to the Edison phonograph during a visit to the ROM.[197]

R.S. Williams Jr., benefited from his efforts and knowledge of both the new technology and the traditions of musical-instrument dealing, and this combined

A class listening to the Edison phonograph, with the original caption from the *Canadian Music Trades Journal*, No. 9, 1919. The picture was taken in front of a staircase in the east side of the old Royal Ontario Museum building, which was demolished during expansion work in 1933. Courtesy National Library of Canada, Music Division, Ottawa, Ontario.

with his business sense put the R.S. Williams & Sons Co. in a very strong position. At the outbreak of World War I, the firm was a highly structured organization, with a well-controlled system of wholesale and retail departments supported by a central advertising body. The vice-president and general manager, H.G. Stanton, governed the firm. In 1914 the custom of inspection of the branches by the general manager was changed, and the branch managers visited their headquarters in Toronto instead, spending a week in conference with officials of the company and departmental managers. The branch managers at that time were C.R. Coleman for Montreal, O. Wagner for Winnipeg, and Charles Clarin for Calgary.[198]

Business connections with Europe were kept alive even at the beginning of the war. John I. Dinsmore returned in February 1915 from a two-month visit to London, Glasgow, and Paris, and reported having successfully completed a number of business contacts. He would not have known, however, about the problems that would arise in England, particularly in the piano industries, which in 1916 were limited by severe government regulations. During this visit there was yet no hint about future drastic measures. In 1917 musical instruments were classified as a restricted industry, allowed an annual output of only about one-fifth the level of pre-war production of new pianos and repair of old ones.[199]

Williams' tradition of sponsoring social events in order to foster good relations among his staff continued; he had organized outings ever since 1907. The tenth annual outing of the firm on June 13, 1918 is well documented. The party sailed on the *Cayuga*, leaving the Yonge Street wharf at 7:30 a.m. for Queenston Heights. Wounded Canadian soldiers were guests of the company. The group pictures of these outings in 1919 and 1920 show the same location, but the photograph of the twelfth outing shows no military persons; it is also the latest photograph discovered which documents these events.

Such details as the inclusion of the soldiers and the programmes for these three outings contribute to our concept of the social history of the City of Toronto and its taste in entertainment. All records of these outings mention entertainment in the form of musical programmes and dances. Perhaps this is what inspired the wholesale division of the R.S. Williams & Sons Co. to found a band of fourteen members.

R.S. Williams' attitude of promoting good fellowship, loyalty, and cooperation in the company is shown particularly in his positive relation with the young employees, especially in their sporting activities. For example, in 1915 Williams was president of the so-called "Bush League," a local baseball league of business houses, and in the first season the "Williams boys" trimmed the *Toronto Star* Players.[200]

During this period, the good name of Williams was upheld significantly by the success of the Oshawa firm. The export trade of the Williams Piano Company in 1916 extended to New Zealand, and in the same year the company shipped an order to Jamaica.[201] Ten years later the company was shipping pianos to South America, Trinidad, Japan, Australia, the Malay States, Singapore, and China. The total exports represented ten percent of the firm's annual business volume. Of all brands of piano, the favourite instruments abroad were the

The Seventh Annual Outing of the Williams firm, July 1914. Courtesy National Library of Canada, Music Division, Ottawa, Ontario.

Williams and the Ennis; of the player pianos the favourites were the Beethoven, Schubert, and Everson models.[202]

Things also appeared bright for R.S. Williams & Sons Co. immediately after World War I. J.A. Hassall, manager of the retail piano department, prepared with his staff the tenth annual piano club sale in February 1919. On the third day they made an announcement to the public, answering concerns about post-war business possibilities during the economic "reconstruction":

"We submit as a barometer to the public generally, that, during the opening of our Tenth Annual Piano Club on Saturday last, and the bona fide sale of 120 pianos to the citizens of Toronto, in a single day, indicates the citizens of Toronto believe as we believe, that if Canada was worth fighting for, she was worth working for, and that this country is settling down to its industry, commerce, and general development. ... We believe the sale of 120 pianos in a single day, in one city, is the biggest piano sale record in the history of Canada. It further shows that the people of Toronto intended to express their appreciation of what their boys have fought for and won, and making this world a better place to live in, through Music in the Home, and, best of all, to add to the education of their children, this inspiring medium. ..."[203]

That the musical education of children was a concern of people in Toronto

96

at the time might suggest that conditions were good, not only for the sale of pianos, but also for the sale of violins that, although only one aspect of the business, remained the centre of interest for R.S. Williams.

The collecting and trade of old violins could not have been maintained at the desired level had Williams not secured the best experts for his violin repair and maintenance departments. This work was headed by a Mr. Dulunet, who came to Williams after resigning a position with W.E. Hill & Sons in London.[204] The second violin maker, attracted from the same London firm, was George Heinl, who worked with Williams from 1912 to 1920. Other specialists were hired by the R.S. Williams firm, among them, S. Berini, who was with the firm for forty-two years.

Then, in 1920, R.S. Williams was fortunate in securing the services of the renowned French violin maker Auguste Delivet.[205] According to R.S. Williams Jr., Delivet made 176 violins, including those which were taken with him from his shop in Paris when he moved to Canada. Williams describes these violins:

"These instruments were all sold by our house at from $500 down as low as $250.00 We have a card index of these specimens, giving date finished and to whom sold. Some of these specimens were made by Vantrum [correct name is Vautrin Joseph, Paris] – a relative; others by Kritzler of Paris, and were varnished by Delivet. Unfortunately, some of his labels, after his death, were sold by his widow to unscrupulous dealers who used them on all sorts of cheap fiddles."[206]

Delivet also made violas and violoncellos

"which were attractive as any of the modern French school; often sought for by connoisseurs in search of instruments of the highest possible

A group of between 200 and 300 public school children studying the violin. This Journal has for long been urging the dealers' interest in promoting instrumental music in the schools.

Picture with its original caption in the *Canadian Music Trades Journal,* No. 2, 1919. Courtesy National Library of Canada, Music Division, Ottawa, Ontario.

skilled workmanship. Very rich oil varnish of various shades. Tone quality remarkably mellow and very very clear."[207]

To the labels of instruments Delivet made in Toronto was added this text: "Made in the workshops of the R.S. Williams & Sons Co. Limited, Toronto, Canada." Delivet's label was ornamented with the design of a violin and bow and with the facsimiles of medals in scrolled work. The instruments produced for the Williams' firm were divided into three classes: the first class, branded "A. Delivet" on the inside and under the saddle above the endpin on the outside, sold for $250; the second for $200; and the third, marked "Sous la Direction" and made by Delivet's assistants, sold for $150.[208] There is some discrepancy, however, between these prices and those listed in the catalogue.[209] Certainly Delivet was a great asset to the firm, supporting the good name of the house and enhancing the reputation of R.S. Williams Jr., as a connoisseur and trader in the world of old and rare violins.

Considering Delivet's output of fine instruments, there is a marked lack of surviving violins. Among the hundreds of instruments brought to the Royal Ontario Museum for examination and identification, from all parts of Canada for fifteen years, not one turned out to be made by Auguste Delivet, or bore his label. However, in the Remenyi House of Music in Toronto, among the more valuable

Certificate issued to Mrs. Charles Edward Pratt of Toronto, with the Delivet violin No. 287. Courtesy Remenyi House of Music, Toronto.

pieces, Michael Remenyi has a few Delivet instruments.

From the year when Auguste Delivet started his work with the firm there are two rare documents revealing that R.S. Williams Jr., was continuing his collector's activities. They are two letters written to Williams by Arthur F. Hill, one in May 1920, and the other in November of the same year.

The second letter mentions two paintings that were acquired by R.S. Williams, and that were kept in his library. The paintings are described as follows: "Dr. Augustine Arne, Mus. Doc. Born 1716, died 1778. Composer of Rule Britannia. Portrait by Gainsborough." (Thomas Augustine Arne was born in 1710.) "Angello Corelly, born 1653, died 1713. Portrait by Howard. Mentioned in *Hawkins History of Music*." (The name of the great violinist and composer was Archangelo Corelli.)[210] These portraits were not included in Williams' gift to the Royal Ontario Museum.

The last paragraph of this letter gives information about the post-war situation in the trade of old violins. The expectation that the war would have a positive influence on the market, and the disappointment when that did not happen, are both expressed by the renowned house of Hill.

Further proof of Williams' passion for collecting is found in letters he exchanged with the Royal Ontario Museum. From them can be seen his dedication to complementing the collection with other irreplaceable objects.

June 1, 1920:
... I am taking the liberty of sending to you direct from London, England, a very fine and interesting piano, as described in the circular enclosed. This will I think be most interesting to the students of the piano.[211]

A letter dated February 11, 1921 to R.S. Williams from the Secretary to the Board of Trustees, Royal Ontario Museum, mentions other additions to the collection:

"At the last meeting of the Board of Trustees of the Royal Ontario Museum the Director of the Department of Archaeology reported your donation of a framed pen-and-ink portrait of Dragonetti, also of a fortepiano (the first piano made in London) by Johannes Zumpe, 1768. The Trustees are very much pleased with these additions to your fine collection and have directed me to convey to you their thanks for the gifts."[212]

On February 1923, R.S. Williams wrote to Dr. Currelly offering another instrument, a "Viola de Amour." This viola d'amore is among the finest specimens in the collection. The label on the inside reads, "Ludovicus Guersan prape Comoediam Gallicam Lutelice Anno 1761."

In 1924 both firms, R.S. Williams & Sons Co. Limited in Toronto and the Williams Piano Company Limited in Oshawa, celebrated the seventy-fifth anniversary of their foundation in 1849. Although the actual year of establishment of the first R.S. Williams' firm in Toronto was 1856, the year 1849, when the founder was only fifteen years of age and apprenticed to Townsend, was used to mark the firm's beginning. The anniversary was opportunity for both firms to remember and pay tribute to those who, under the name of Williams, had contributed so much to the development of the Canadian music industry. Part of the documentation of this event is a series of portraits of officers and workers who had long years of service with the two firms. Most of them had worked under the founder, R.S. Williams, Sr., and under his eldest son Robert:

> "Although Mr. Williams [Robert] had the misfortune to be a partial invalid for a number of years, he still takes a keen interest in the affairs of Oshawa, and is always interested to receive visits from members of the piano trade, and to hear of the changes that have taken place."[213]

The anniversary underlined the important role of the Williams' family in pioneering and building the Canadian music industry – manufacturing, trade, and commerce. The future of the Williams' firm seemed secure. The two businesses appeared strong enough to withstand the competition that existed under the post-war economic and social conditions.

The Canadian music industry was fortunate in not being subject to biting government regulations and consequent restrictions and limitations on manufacturing, such as those imposed in England during the war. Profits here

Group photograph of the Williams Piano Company Ltd. employees in Oshawa, 1924. Courtesy Mr. Th. Bouckley, Oshawa, Ontario.

seemed sufficient to keep the business progressing. There are no sources or documents providing evidence that the R.S. Williams & Sons Co. Limited in Toronto was on a different course from the industry in general. On the contrary, the six years after World War I brought the expected prosperity.

However, the Williams' family suffered a great loss when Sarah, the widow of R.S. Williams, Sr., died in 1926, and other unfortunate events followed. Among the records in a family New Testament these deaths are noted: on January 5, 1927 Robert Williams; on May 9, 1927 his wife Mazo. Auguste Delivit died of heart failure at the Toronto Exhibition in September 1927.

A month later R.S. Williams & Sons Co. Limited declared bankruptcy; a Notice to Creditors was posted on October 1, 1927.[214] None of the available sources hints at the reason for the sudden collapse of the Toronto firm. Memories of the event cannot be authenticated because of lack of documentation. The sudden change in the situation of R.S. Williams Jr., and the business of which he was president was recorded, however, in the Toronto media.

Under the expressive title "R.S. Williams Company Limited is Achievement of Pioneer Work Which Dates Back to Year 1849," is news of the birth of a new "Williams" business without the Williamses. The article's lengthy introduction is actually a short biography, sometimes inaccurate, of R.S. Williams, Sr., the founder of the original firm. The tone shows the desire of the new owners to take advantage of the firm's prestigious past:

"For many years Mr. Williams was the acknowledged head of the music industry in Canada, and it is a noteworthy fact that practically any executive in the music industry

R.S. Williams employees of many years service, with captions from the *Canadian Music Trades Journal*, No. 4, 1924. Courtesy National Library of Canada, Music Division, Ottawa, Ontario.

today received his early training in the Williams organization. Following the death of Mr. Williams in 1905 [sic], the business was successfully and capably managed by his son, Mr. Williams Jr. until its sale to Messrs. B.A. and F.A. Trestrail in February, 1928. An interesting touch of romance is lent to this business transaction by the fact that Mr. B.A. Trestrail, the President of the new company, began as Advertising Manager under R.S. Williams Jr. in 1912, and was successively Manager of the Piano Department and Manager of Sales and Promotion. Mr. F.A. Trestrail, the Vice-President of the new company, was also indirectly associated with the old business through his connections with the Williams Piano Company of Oshawa."[215]

The article states that a completely new decorating scheme throughout the entire Williams' building would make it one of the finest and most modern music stores in North America. However, the most essential change made by the new owners is indicated in the last paragraph of the article:

"In preparing for the formal Opening of the new store, all used instruments are being cleared from the floors to makes room for thousands of dollars' worth of new merchandise, including such famous lines as the Rogers-Batteryless and Majestic electric radios, Ortho-phonic Victrolas and Victor V.E. records; Knabe, Chickering, Willis, Ampico, Wurlitzer and Ennis pianos; Conn, Ludwig, Martin, Deagan and Pan-American small instruments."[216]

Gone was the trade in old instruments that for two generations had contributed to the fine Williams' collection.

Another article, entitled "Two Makers of Radio at R.S. Williams Co.," discloses the main programme of the "new business under the old name." B.A. and F.A. Trestrail reorganized the radio department, the youngest component of the original firm; they wanted to offer to the public the best radio in the world, backed with twenty-four hour service, and to develop the largest retail radio business in Canada. As the best product they selected the Rogers-Batteryless and the Majestic electric radios as "conceived, created, developed and perfected in Canada."[217]

The new owners at first seemed eager to gain as much as possible from the tradition and name of Williams. The formal opening of the new store of the R.S. Williams Company prompted an article entitled "First organs in Canada made in R.S. Williams store":

"One of the policies of the R.S. Williams Company which is responsible to a great extent at least for its popularity is the determination to keep for the benefit of their customers a diversified stock which covers the entire musical field."[218]

The Globe published a portrait of R.S. Williams, Sr., reproduced from a photograph of the late 1890s, with the caption, "R.S. Williams, the late founder of the R.S. Williams Company, Limited."

But it was not long before the philosophy of the new owners began to assert itself. The final end of the Williams' tradition in the Canadian manufacture of musical instruments came two years after the sale of the business, in October 1930. After a clearing sale of musical instruments, the R.S. Williams Company, Limited, became a household specialty shop, although it still occupied the proud ten-storey building with the lyre emblem and the initials "R S W" at the top.

Meanwhile the Williams' music business did continue, in the form of General Musical Supplies, Limited, which opened in Toronto with a branch in Winnipeg, as "Successors to the Wholesale Division of the R.S. Williams & Sons Co., Limited." The location of this firm was listed as 145 Yonge Street and 468 King Street West. A memorandum to the office of the Deputy Provincial Registrar from the Assistant Provincial Secretary dated Toronto, 19 October 1937, disclosed the changes of name under which the original Toronto company continued until the 1950s, although only as a warehouse operation:

> "This company has been fully wound up voluntarily under the Companies Act, and its original Letters Patent, Supplementary Letter Patent and one Order changing the name of the Company have been returned to this office, but the second Order cannot be located.
>
> The Letters Patent, issued under the name "General Musical Merchandise, Limited", bear the date April 25, A.D., 1928, and were recorded as Number 30 in Liber 228.
>
> The Supplementary Letters Patent bear the date October 2, A.D., 1928, and were recorded as Number 105 in Liber 25.
>
> An order-in-Council, changing the corporate name to "General Musical Supplies, Limited," bears the date October 11, A.D., 1928.
>
> By Order of the Provincial Secretary, dated April 1, A.D., 1931, the corporate name was changed to the R.S. Williams & Son Company, Limited."[219]

In the Letters Patent of April 26, 1928, the merchandise carried by General Musical Supplies is listed, including "Cameras and parts of the same and camera equipment, radio-talking-moving picture equipment and sporting goods of all kinds."[220]

In these same years the Williams Piano Company in Oshawa also underwent great changes.

> "Williams went into the radio business and in three years became the 7th largest manufacturer of radios in Canada. To keep the hands employed winter and summer Williams started to build canoes and rowboats and was ahead of his time in building sea-fleas."[221]

The proud days of piano making were over.

> "The Williams' company was producing heterodyne radios, ten and eleven-tube sets, and disaster struck with the invention of the super-heterodyne five-, six- or seven-tube sets. De Forest-Crossley and Rogers-Majestic went bankrupt; the Williams company lost seventy-five thousand dollars in that year.
>
> The Depression was closing in, and in 1931 the "Piano Works" as it was always called, closed."[222]

11

A WORLD OF MUSIC HISTORY (1927-1945)

R.S. Williams Jr. – connoisseur, collector, and music lover to the very end.

The bankruptcy and sale of R.S. Williams & Sons Co. Limited in Toronto in 1927-1928, and the closing of the Williams Piano Company Limited in Oshawa in 1931 marked the end of the Williamses' involvement in musical-instrument manufacturing. "My father wasn't the same person after it happened,"[223] recalled Mrs. Isobel W. Brock, youngest daughter of R.S. Williams Jr., talking about the years 1927 and 1928.

General Musical Supplies, Limited, issued their Catalogue No. 1 on November 1, 1928. Beneath the firm's name is the information that it is the "Successor to the Wholesale Division of the R.S. Williams & Sons Co., Limited, 143 Yonge Street, Toronto 2, Canada, Branch – Winnipeg, Man." Obviously the catalogue had been prepared for the defunct firm, as indicated by the format, design, and arrangement of the merchandise. The section on violins begins with its own introduction and with the well-known picture of the violinist listening to his tuning fork. One page of the catalogue is dedicated to Auguste Delivet, with the information that just before his death he had completed orders for "Violins for such renowned artists as Fritz Kreisler, Elman, Press, Thibaud and Casals."[224] Under the picture of Lord Aylesford's Stradivari violin of 1683 is the following text:

"These reproductions are made by master artisans from the finest material obtainable, and are minutely copied – every detail direct from the famous Lord Aylesford Stradivari, which was formerly the property of our president, Mr. R.S. Williams."[225]

The instrument must have been copied in 1914 during the very short time it was owned by R.S. Williams Jr.

Although the family business was gone, R.S. Williams Jr., kept the spirit of his father alive in his devotion to collecting. Despite mental and physical hardship, which vexed him around this time, he continued to assert his expert knowledge in active work. A pamphlet published by General Musical Supplies looks as if it were issued by the late house of R.S. Williams & Sons. Over the title "Is My Violin a Genuine Stradivari" is again the familiar figure of the violinist listening to his tuning fork.

The folding pages of this pamphlet contain an article signed "R.S. Williams, violin Expert and Collector." It begins, "In this little pamphlet it is my desire to try to assist the amateur collector and lovers of the 'king of instruments' to more fully understand the earmarks of the work of the old master violin makers."[226] Then follows a brief, general history of Williams' collecting activities with a paragraph about the collecting and connoisseurship of his father. Finally there is a discussion of the characteristics of violins of the various schools. A second, much shorter article deals with the repair of violins under the title "The restoring of valuable violins." It is part of an advertisement, and is "signed" by the firm, not by Williams himself. Its third paragraph has this information: "Our repair department is under the direct supervision of Mr. R.S. Williams, the noted violin expert and collector, and is fully equipped with the most modern tools and appliances that experience and money can buy."[227]

Our supposition about the dating of this pamphlet is based on letterhead of the firm used February 13, 1932: "The R.S. Williams & Son Co. Limited, General Musical Supplies, 468 King Street West, Toronto 2." In the upper left corner is printed, "R.S. Williams, President. A. L. Robertson, Vice-President and General Manager." The letter is from Williams' correspondence with Dr. Currelly at the Royal Ontario Museum. In the following year the same letterhead appeared without R.S. Williams identified as President in the upper left corner. Thus the pamphlet can be dated as of 1933.

The continuing correspondence with the Royal Ontario Museum proves as well R.S. Williams' never-ceasing interest in his collection. Suddenly, however, after more than ten years of friendly collaboration and understanding, there appears a letter from Williams expressing bitterness and disappointment about certain plans for displaying the collection.

This brought a soothing reply the next day from Dr. Currelly suggesting that a room full of pianos would look rather forbidding, and on April 29, 1933, Williams continued the correspondence with his own enthusiastic views about the use of his collection:

"Sorry to hear that my views did not agree with yours, but with all your experience I still think you are wrong. I, personally, have visited a great many Museums in the old land, as well as in America but I cannot recall one where Musical Instruments are displayed as you propose.

The principal use of this collection is for the education of musical students, and this use is defeated by the fact that the instruments are not together so that they can be compared and the points of difference shown by the teacher. If you will give me an idea of when you will be at the Museum, I will call and talk over the matter with you." [228]

Actually, the aims of the generous donor had never really been at variance with those of the Museum. The clouds and storms raised by temporary misunderstandings disappeared with the opening of the new wing of the museum in 1933, as attested by Dr. Currelly's letter to R.S. Williams on the very eve of the opening:

"The decision of the Board that the Museum must be reopened at such an early date has meant that we have had about seven months to arrange seventy galleries. You can understand the mad scramble it has been to get things into an even presentable condition, and it will be several months before we can have all our permanent cases made and the galleries completed. I trust you will not be displeased with the way your collection is exhibited, considering that it is a temporary arrangement. If you will arrange a time that suits you to come in to help us with the permanent arrangement, we shall be tremendously grateful. I hope we shall have a pleasure of seeing you here tomorrow at the official opening."[229]

The next day, October 12, 1933, brought this letter from R.S. Williams to Dr. Currelly:

"I think you have done wonders in the short time the Directors allowed you. I will be delighted to assist you in the arrangement of my Collection. I have a few sujestions [sic] that I think will be helpful, and I have some other instruments to add to my Collection which I think will be interesting to the Publick [sic]. If you will arrange a date I will be pleased to spend what ever time is necessary with you to arrange the collection to the best advantage."[230]

So the ice was broken, and the former harmony restored. Later letters serve to emphasize the generous

The Dancing Master, 1706.

Les cent cinquante Pseaumes de David by Claude le Jeune, 1650.

motives of the connoisseur, who wanted his collection to be a resource for anyone at all who had an interest in music.

In 1934 Williams supplemented his gift of instruments, rare music scores, and books with a collection of 290 autograph letters and documents of famous personalities of the world of music. There is so far no evidence of his father's participation in forming this collection; it appears to be exclusively the result of his own endeavours.

The papers are important and Williams amassed this part of his collection with care; this was no incidental sideline to the collection of instruments. Emphasizing the life of music in England at the end of the eighteenth and throughout the nineteenth centuries, the collector seems to have been inspired by the idea of creating a collection of first-hand historical information that would give a picture of the musical culture of England. The nature and focus on this part of the collection were influenced by the fact that the Williams' family was of English extraction, and that the widespread traditions of music in Toronto were rooted in English music.

The usefulness of the autograph collection is evident. For instance, a letter written in 1785 by Dr. Charles Burney, composer and author of the well-known *General History of Music*, is of interest to anyone eager to know the historical background of the Irish harp as

K. Czerny: Rondo III, fragment.

the symbol on the arms of Ireland. Letters from Williams Crotch, Doctor of Music, tell of the foundation of the Royal Academy of Music, of which he was the first principal. No less interesting are his reports on pupils who studied harmony with him in 1828. Many of them, such as Charles Lucas, Thomas Mudie, and Williams Holmes, became leading English musicians.

Among the autographs of musical personalities are those of English virtuoso performers such as Thomas Attwood (a pupil of Mozart), Sir John Frederick Bridge, and Arabella Goddard. Features of musical life in England are illustrated by autographs of famous musicians and performers – notably Mario, Giulia Grisi, Malibran, and Lind – on letters to the manager of Covent Garden Theatre. Other autograph letters are by Beethoven, Berlioz, Czerny, Donizetti, Dragonetti, Flotow, Gounod, Halevy, Leschetizky, Mendelssohn-Bartholdy, Paderewski, Paganini, Anton Gregor Rubinstein, Clara Schumann, Suppe, Verdi, and Wagner. Even if the letters are not of such importance as some in other great collections, they still breathe the spirit of a glorious time in the development of music. This collection, together with the music scores and books donated in 1913, is a fine complement to the collection of musical instruments.

The collection of musical scores includes the works of such great musicians as Purcell and Handel, the former represented by a seventeenth century edition of *Orpheus Britannicus*, the latter by Samuel Arnold's 1786 edition of Handel's works in forty volumes. Among the church music is a 1714 edition of *Harmonia Sacra or Divine Hymns and Dialogues*, and *Les Cent Cinquante Pseaumes de David* by Claude le Jeune, printed in Paris in 1650. Secular music is represented by such works as *The New Ayres and Dialogues* by John Banister and Thomas Low, printed in London in 1678, and a thirteenth edition of *The Dancing Master*, London, 1706. There is also some well-known educational music, including *Forty-two Suites of Lessons for the Harpsichord* by D. Scarlatti, and G. Tartini's *The Art of the Bow for the Violin*.

The years 1935 and 1936 were the last in which R.S. Williams added musical instruments to the collection in the Royal Ontario Museum. The last of his letters about his collection accompanied a gift of five instruments, of which the most valuable were the late eighteenth century English timpani.

Few documents exist to give us a picture of the next eight years in the life of R.S. Williams Jr. And yet, thanks to his youngest daughter, Isobel Brock, two last letters from his correspondence with the Hills in London are preserved. Particularly the letter of May 22, 1944 tells of the last years of the Hills' one-time friend and business partner, and draws a picture of the "business in the violin world" of the time.

"I am in receipt of your letter of the 22nd ult. and thank you for the remittance contained therein in payment of our book on the Guarneri Family, receipt for which and requisite declaration forms are enclosed herewith; the book has been duly posted to you and I hope it will reach you safely and its possession, afford you pleasure.

The loss of my late partners, Messrs. Arthur & Alfred Hill within so short a speace of each other, was indeed a bitter blow and entailed many difficulties in a very trying time. I am glad to say, however, that we have managed to carry on our business satisfactorily; and at the same time, meet all our obligations, more especially those accuring from my late partners' respective estates which, in these days of high taxation, were by no means light!

Mr. George Hart whose widow I occasionally see, has also disappeared from the fiddle world, and his step-brother, Herbert Hart has given up business and retired to the country and I very much doubt his re-establishing himself after the war.

Charles Hill, on whom you so kindly kept an eye when he was in Canada, returned to England after the last war. ...

You mention Mr. Edison, the great inventor, which interests me, inasmuch as a member of my wife's family, a Mr. Goold, was associated with him, many years ago, and I am wondering if, perchance he is still alive and, if you can tell me anything about him.

Business in the violin world has been quite brisk in England within recent years, in fact, there has been quite a revival in violin-playing during the war, no doubt, to the absence of other diversions!

The parcels of food you so kindly sent in the early years of the war, were duly forwarded to the widows of my late partners and I am sorry to learn that their letters failed to reach you, for I have no doubt that they would have acknowledged them forthwith; those alas were the days when enemy submarines were playing havoc with our shipping!

I am glad to hear such good accounts of your son: should he ever come over here again; I shall be delighted to see him. My son is engaged on much the same sort of work in the Mediterranean. He was trained as a violin-maker and, before the outbreak of hostilities, was my right-hand man consequently. I am eagerly looking forward to the time when he can resume his peace-time occupation!

With my best wishes for your future welfare,
I am
Very truly yours
A. Phillips Hill"[231]

Certainly the troubled time at which these letters were exchanged was not the twilight of the violin industry or of the rest of the musical-instrument trade. But it was the last year of the life of R.S. Williams Jr. Even at seventy years of age he still longed for more knowledge about his favourite instrument, and bought a book on the Guarneri family directly from the authors, the Hills.

Perhaps he needed the book to fulfill a long-standing wish: "I hope in the near future to publish an illustrated catalogue of my collection of antique musical instruments and autograph letters of musical celebrities in the Royal Ontario Museum."[232] Or he might have planned to use it to summarize his lifelong dedication to musical instruments as a means of advancing musical culture in Canada. Whatever his intention, there was no time for him to realize it. He died on March 24, 1945:

The burial place and monument of the R.S. Williams family in Mount Pleasant Cemetery, Toronto, Ontario.

"The memory of Richard Sugden Williams, lifelong businessman of Toronto in the music trade, who died last Saturday, will be perpetuated in this city by his wonderful gift to the Royal Ontario Museum of a large collection of ancient musical instruments. ... There is a world of music history wrapped up in this generous gift."[233]

EPILOGUE

Until recently many people passed by without noticing the tiny "skycraper" at 145 Yonge Street in downtown Toronto. Perhaps some pondered the unusual lyre and trumpet emblem and the initials "R S W." Few knew, however, that the building was a kind of monument to R.S. Williams, Sr., and to the family that contributed so much to the development of musical life in Toronto and in Canada. The R.S. Williams Building, erected in 1912, and 143 Yonge Street, one of the buildings in which the Williams' business operated soon after its establishment in 1856, were demolished in 1985.

Very similar has been the fate of other sites that might have reminded us of stages in the growth of the Williams' enterprise. The Toronto *Globe and Mail* in 1954 reported the destruction of the fine home of R.S. Williams, Sr., at the corner of Wellesley and Sherbourne Streets. In 1917 this house was still the residence of Sarah, the widow of R.S. Williams, Sr.;[234] Mrs. I.W. Brock, daughter of R.S. Williams Jr., has said that her grandmother lived there until her death in 1926.

A 1970 article dramatically describes the demolition of the Williams' pipe-organ and piano plant in Oshawa: "The demolition squad has just about finished its work, and soon the old 'Piano Works", as it was familiarly known, will have disappeared to make way for a new Police Station."[235] No trace was left of the site where organs and pianos had been built for so many years.

In 1945, R.S. Williams Jr., the last member of the family to carry on the tradition of musical-instrument manufacture established by his father eighty-nine years earlier, was buried in the family plot in Mount Pleasant Cemetery near the entrance on Yonge Street. He was buried beside his father and mother, and his brother Robert. Also buried there were the other children of R.S. Williams, Sr. – Frank, Richard, and Henrietta – all of whom had died before R.S. Williams Jr., was born.

The real legacy of the Williams family, however, is not a building or a family cemetery marker, but rather the contribution to the musical-instrument business and to the musical life of Canada. The Williamses were active at that crucial time when locally made instruments were just beginning to compete with imports. In those early years, the Williamses shared with other firms the establishment of the new industry and the nurturing of the public's interest in music through education and entertainment.

In this work I have endeavoured to present and assess the accomplishments of the Williams family. To do this it has been necessary to contend with a scarcity of sources and with sometimes uncritical, sometimes naïve exaggerations of their role as businessmen and as connoisseurs of fine musical instruments. In all of this, however, the achievement of the Williams family stands as a unique and lasting testimony of their dedication and ability.

APPENDIX A
Patents for Piano Improvements and Attachments

Below is a selected list of patents for improvements and attachments for the piano, dating from 1844 to 1872. Patent numbers are included, as are page references to the list (*List of Canadian Patents*).

No. 71. Milligan, George, of Quebec for a "New method of constructing Piano Fortes." Montreal, November 21, 1844, p. 6.

No. 78. Warren, Samuel R., of Montreal for a "Method of constructing Harmonic Attachments for Piano Fortes." Montreal, July 9, 1845, p. 6.

No. 163. Thomas, John Morgan, and Smith, Alexander of the City of Toronto, for "A new improvement in the construction of Piano Fortes, by means of which their durability is much prolonged, and the tone of the instrument preserved." Toronto, March 23, 1840, p. 10.

No. 306. Mead, George Hooper, of the City of Montreal, for "An improved method of constructing Piano Fortes." Toronto, January 8, 1851, p. 16.

No. 525. Hood, Thomas, D., of the City of Montreal, for "A new and improved method of constructing that part of the Pianoforte called the Hopper." Quebec, August 10, 1855, p. 26.

No. 913. Matthews, William, of City of Toronto, in the Country of York, for "A Metallic equal tension plate for Cottage Piano Fortes." Toronto, February 9, 1859, p. 44.

No. 1239. Thomas, John, of City of Toronto, in County of York, for "An improvement in the construction of the Piano Forte." Quebec, May 21, 1861, p. 58.

No. 1899. Fox, Conrad, of the City of Kingston, in the County of Frontenac, for "An improved Sounding Board for Pianos." Quebec, September 23, 1865, p. 89.

No. 2098. Rainer, Joseph Frederick, of the Town of Whitby, in the County of Ontario, for "A new and useful Style of Piano, known as Rainer's new Elliptic Piano." Ottawa, September 13, 1866, p. 99.

No. 2654. Rainer, Joseph Frederick, of the Town of Whitby, in the County of Ontario, for "Certain new and useful improvements in the Piano Forte, for the better arrangement of the scale, the increasing of the power, and the securing the greater durability of the tune therefore, to be called Rainer's New Dominion Grand Piano." Ottawa, June 26, 1868, p. 128.

No. 2888. Craig, James Peter, of the City of Montreal, in the District of Montreal, for "Certain new and useful improvements to be called Piano systeme Craig." Ottawa, December 4, 1868, p. 142.

This section of the list ends with No. 3325, and the new section starts under the heading "Patents issued for five years, under

Patent Act of 1869." While the pagination continues, the numbering of the patents starts anew.

No. 323. G.W. Scribner, of Chatham, Ont., for "Improvement in Reed Organs," Ottawa, March 29, 1870, p. 172.

No. 1496. S.R. Warren, Montreal, Que., "Improvements in the construction of Organs." June 1, 1872, p. 218.

No. 1578. T. Kater, Hamilton, Ont., "Improvements in Pianos." August 3, 1872, p. 220.

APPENDIX B
Toronto Directory Listings for 1892

By 1892 the Toronto music industry was advancing through the growing popularity of the piano. Even more remarkable than the increased number of piano manufacturers listed in city directories is the number of auxiliary industries that appear at this time; in addition to the companies listed as auxiliary to the piano industry, Toronto had nine independent piano tuners in 1892.

The list of organ manufacturers includes both piano and organ manufacturers: the list below identifies those companies that do not appear as piano manufacturers, but only as makers of organs. Note that, as in previous Toronto Directories, only one manufacturer of organ reeds is listed. It is clear that while the number of piano manufacturers and related industries was increasing, the organ industry remained relatively stable. (All listings, TD 1892.)

Piano Manufacturers
Anglo Colonia Mnfg. Co., 108 King w.; Barthelmes, F.L. 541 King w.; Bell Organ & Piano Co. (LTD), 70 King w.; Coulter, Joseph, 102 Adelaide w.; Gerhard Heintzman Co., Factory and Warerooms: 60 to 75 Sherbourne Street, Telephone 1636. City Sales Room - 188 Yonge Street; Heintzman & Co. 117 King w.; Hoerr H. & F., 201 Queen e.; Mason & Risch, 32 King w.; Newcombe Octavius & Co.; 107-109 Church; Nordheimer Mnfg. Co. (LDT) 86 York; Owen, R.S., 23 D'Arcy; Schumann Piano Co., 75 Queen s.; Williams R.S. & Son, 143 Yonge.

Auxiliary Industries
Piano actions
Barthelmes A.A. & Co., 91 Niagara; Koth Frederick, 91 Richmond s.

Piano hardware
Dorrien Plating and Mnfg. Co., 99 Adelaide w.

Piano keys
Loose, M., 105 Niagara; Wagner, Zeidler & Co., Toronto Junction.

Piano hammers
Bohne W. & Co., 91 Niagara.

Piano strings
Coates A.E., 33 Richmond e.

Piano stools
Smith W.P. & Co., 106 Adelaide w.

Organ Manufacturers (apart from Piano Manufacturers) Lye Edward & Sons, w.s. St. Nicholas, corn. Phipps; Nordheimer A. & S., 15 King e.; Warren S.R. & Son, 39-47 McMurich.

Organ Reeds
Newell & Co., 31 Hayter Street.

Piano and Organ Dealers
Andrews W. a., 124 Adelaide e.; Bell Organ & Piano Co. (LTD), 70 King w.; Button a. T. & Co., 107 Yonge; Dominion Piano & Organ Co., 68 King w.; Courlay, Winter & Leeming,

188 Yonge; Gardner J.A., 594 Yonge; Heintzman Gerhard Co., 69-75 Sherbourne; Heintzman & Co., 117 King w.; McSpadden Wm., 64 King w.; Mason & Risch, 32 King w. and 653 Queen w.; Newcombe Octavius & Co., 107-109 Church; Nordheimer A. & S., 15 King e.; Suckling J. & Sons, 107 Yonge; Toronto Musical Instrument Co., 346 Queen w.; Uxbridge Piano Co., 107 Yonge; Webster George, 507 1/2 Yonge; Williams R.S. & Son, 143 Yonge.

Music and Musical Instruments
Billing W.H., 67 Yonge; Butland Mrs. E., 37 King w.; Claxton Thomas, 197 Yonge; Corlett Edmund, 340 Yonge; Galster J.F., 275 King e.; Hugill Joseph (Violins), 304 Wilton ave.; Nordheimer, A. & S., 15 King e,; Paye Wm., 409 Queen w.; Reichers Albert, Violin Maker and Repairer, Dealer in String instruments, Strings, Bows, etc., 4 McCaul Street; Suckling J. & Sons, 107 Yonge; Whaley, Royce & Co., 158 Yonge; Williamson W.C., 1044 Queen w.; Wood Littleton, 208 Richmond w.

Music Publishers and Dealers
Alexander W.H. & Co., 12 King e.; anglo-Canadian Music Publishers Assn., 68 King w.; Billing W.H., 67 Yonge; Buttland Mrs. E., 37 King w.; Claxton Thomas, 197 Yonge; Corlett Edmund, 340 Yonge; Cox A. & Co., 5 Richmond w.; Gourlay, Winter & Leeming, 188 Yonge; Imrie & Graham, 26 Colborne; Nordheimer A. & A., 15 King e.; Payne Wm., 409 Queen w.; Pugh, Mrs. Fanny, 988 Queen w.; Shaw W.F. & Co., 12 Johnson; Strange & Co., 130 King w.; Suckling I & Sons, 107 Yonge; Sutherland James, 232 Yonge; Toronto Musician Instruments Company, 346 Queen w.; Warwood James, 1136 Queen w.; Whaley, Royce & Co. 158 Yonge.

APPENDIX C
Organ Specifications Midland Organ Specifications

(According to Mr. Dieter Geissler, President of Keates-Geissler Pipe Organs Ltd. in Acton, Ontario, who was responsible for the restoration.)

Great Organ
1. Open Diapason — 8 ft.
2. Melodia — 8 ft.
3. Dulciana — 8 ft.
4. Principal — 4 ft.
5. Fifteenth — 2 ft.

Swell Organ
6. Stopped Diapsaon — 8 ft.
7. Violoncello — 8 ft.
8. Harmonic Flute — 4 ft.
9. Oboe (French type double nut) — 8 ft.

Pedal Organ
10. Bourdon — 16 ft.

Couplers
1. Great to Pedal
2. Swell to Pedal
3. Swell to Great

St. Paul's Organ Specifications

Great Organ
1. Open Diapason — 8 ft.
2. Dulciana — 8 ft.
3. Salicional — 8 ft.
4. Melodia — 8 ft.
5. Principal — 4 ft.
6. Flute d'amour — 4 ft.
7. Twelfth — 3 ft.
8. Mixture
9. Trumpet — 8 ft.

Small Organ
1. Concert Flute — 8 ft.
2. Stopped Diapason — 8 ft.
3. Aeoline — 8 ft.
4. Open Diapason — 8 ft.
5. Bourdon — 16 ft.
6. Oboe & Bassoon — 8 ft.
7. Harmonic Piccolo — 2 ft.
8. Violina — 4 ft.
9. Harmonic Flute — 4 ft.
10. Vox Celeste — 8 ft.
11. Vox Humana — 8 ft.

Pedal Organ
12. Bourdon — 16 ft.
13. Open Diapason — 16 ft.

Couplers
1. Great to Pedal
2. Swell to Pedal
3. Swell to Great

Swell Box
1. Swell 2 pistons
2. Great 3 pistons
3. Great to Pedal reversible

St. John's (Cayuga) Organ Specifications

Great Organ
1. Fifteenth — 2 ft.
2. Principal — 4 ft.
3. Dulciana — 8 ft.
4. Melodia — 8 ft.
5. Open Diapason — 8 ft.

Swell Organ
6. Stopped Diapason — 8 ft.
7. Viola — 8 ft.
8. Harmonic Flute — 4 ft.
9. Gamba — 8 ft.

Tremolo Pedal Organ
10. Bourdon — 16 ft.

Couplers
1. Great to Pedal
2. Swell to Pedal
3. Swell to Great

Calgary Organ Specifications
(As given in *The Albertan*, Saturday, June 8, 1968, p. 21. Clipping courtesy of Elwyn S. Davies.)
Pedal: 27 nots; Bourdon 16'; Great to Pedal; Swell to Pedal;Great: 58 notes; Open Diapason 8", Melodia bass 8', Melodia Treable 8', Principal 4'; Swell to Great Octave; Swell: 58 notes, Stopped Diapason Bass 8', Stopped Diapason Treble 8', Viola 8', Harmonic Flute 4', Oboe 8'; Tremolo; Bellows Signal.

APPENDIX D
The Publication of Sheet Music

Although the bulk of the publishing business carried out by the R.S. Williams firm was the production of catalogues, between 1878 and almost 1920 the firm published sheet music as an auxiliary service to their manufacture and dealership in musical instruments. The covers of the sheets that have been preserved are typical of the period, some printed in colour lithograph, with the names of the authors as well as the type of music specified. A1-A4

Courtesy of the Metropolitan Toronto Library Board A5

Courtesy of the National Library of Canada, Music Division A6

Courtesy of the Metropolitan Toronto Library BoardSelected Bibliography AMB

Alte Meistergeigen Beschreibunge, Expertisen [Bd] III, IV, *Die Cremoneser Schule, Antonius Stradivarius*. Frankfurt am Main, 1979. Amtmann 1975

Amtmann, Willy. *Music in Canada* 1600-1800. Montreal, 1975. Andrews 1953

Andrews, Robert E. Gasparo Bertolotti da Saló: *A Brief Account of his Life and of Some of the Instruments he Made*. Berkeley, 1953.

Apprenticeship in Canada *Apprenticeship in Canada, Past and Present*. Washington D.C., 1950; reprinted in Bulletin of the Department of Labour, Ottawa, 1951. Arthur 1974

Arthur, Eric Ross. *Toronto: No Mean City*. Toronto, 1974. Aslin 1962

Aslin, Elizabeth. *Nineteenth Century English Furniture*. London, 1962. Bessaraboff 1941

Bessaraboff, Nicholas. *Ancient European Musical Instruments: An Organological Study of the Instruments in the Leslie Lindsay Mason Collection at the Museum of Fine Arts, Boston*. Cambridge, Mass., 1941; reprint 1964. Boalch 1956

Boalch, D.H. *Makers of the Harpsichord and Clavichord, 1440 to 1840*. London, 1956. Bouckley 1975-1976

Bouckley, Thomas. *Pictorial Oshawa*. 2 vols. Oshawa, Ont., 1975-1976. Britten 1914

Britten [pseud.]. "Renaissance of the viola d'amore." *The Canadian Journal of Music* 1,3 (July-August 1914):49, 54. Buchner 1952

Buchner, A. Catalogue – *Exhibition of Musical Instruments, Prague National Museum*, 1950. Prague, 1952. Buchner 1955

Buchner, A. *Musical Instruments Through the Ages*. I. Irwin, trans. London, 1955. Buckley 1965

Buckley, K.A.H., ed. *Historical Statistics of Canada*. Toronto, 1965.Cameron and

Bruce 1973

Cameron, R., and E. Bruce. "There's an Organ in the Parlour: A Brief History of the Reed Organ in Canada." In *Antiques in Ontario: Canadian Antiques Yearbook*. 5th ed., D. and P. Unitt, comps., 171-78. Peterborough, Ont. 1973. Carrothers 1929

Carrothers, W.A. *Emigration from the British Isles*. London, 1929. Calssey 1968

Classey, Timothy. "Reed Organs in Canada" MS. Toronto, 1968.

CMTJ
Canadian Music and Trade Journal, Toronto, 1900-1907
Canadian Music and Trade Journal, Toronto, 1907-1932.

Commemorative Biographical Record
Commemorative Biographical Record of the County of York, Ontario. Toronto, 1907.

Common Schools
Common Schools in Upper Canada, Annual Report 1845-1846. Montreal, 1847. Cowan 1928

Cowan, Helen I. *British Emigration to British America, 1783-1837*. Toronto, 1928; revised 1961. Cselenyi 1971

Cselenyi, Ladislav. *Musical Instruments in the Royal Ontario Museum*. Toronto, 1971. Cselenyi 1972

Cselenyi, Ladislav. "The Mirror of Music in the ROM: The R.S. Williams Collection." *Rotunda* 5, 3 (Summer 1972): 16-25. Dolge 1911

Dolge, Alfred. *Pianos and Their Makers*. Covina, Calif., 1911; reprint New York, 1972.

Earl Aylesford
"Earl of Aylesford Stradivari, A.D. 1683." *Canadian Journal of Music*, 2, 11 (March 1916): 206. Ehrlich 1976

Ehrlich, C. *The Piano, a History*. London, 1976. Farga 1950

Farga, F. *Violins and Violinists*. London, 1950. Farmer 1912

Farmer, H.G. *The Rise and Development of Military Music*. London, 1912. Firth 1966

Firth, Edith G. *The Town of York 1815-1834*. Toronto, 1966. Firth 1961

Firth, Edith G. ed. *Early Toronto Newspapers 1793-1867*. Toronto, 1961. Galpin 1937

Galpin, Francis W. *A Textbook of European Musical Instruments*. London, 1937. Gardiner Scrapbook

Gardiner, H.F. Scrapbook of Clippings. The Corporation of Hamilton Public Library, Hamilton, Ont. Geiringer 1943

Geiringer, K. *Musical Instruments*. London, 1943; New York, 1945. Gellerman 1973

Gellerman, R.F. *The American Reed Organ*. Vestal, N.Y., 1973.

Great Exhibition
Great Exhibition of the Works of All Nations. 3 vols. London, 1851. Grove Dictionary

Grove, George, Sir. *A Dictionary of Music and Musicians*. 2nd ed., vol. 1., J.A. Fuller Maitland, ed. London, 1904. Guillet 1933

Guillet, Edwin C. *Early Life in Canada*. Toronto, 1933. Hamma 1964

Hamma, W. *Meister italienischer Geigenbaukunst*. Stuttgart, 1964. Hammerich 1911

Hammerich, Angul. *Das Musikhistorische Museum zu Kopenhagen, Beschreibender Katalog*. Copenhagen, 1911. Harding 1933

Harding, R.E.M. *The Piano-Forte: Its History Traced to the Great Exhibition of 1851*. Cambridge, 1933; reprint New York, 1973. Harrison and Rimmer 1964

Harrison, F., and J. Rimmer. *European Musical Instruments*. London, 1964. Hart 1978

Hart, George. *The Violin: Its Famous Makers and Their Imitators*. London, 1885; reprint New York, 1978. Haweis

Haweis, H.R. *Old Violins and Violin Lore*. London, n.d. (1893?). Henley 1959-1969

Henley, William. *Universal Dictionary of Violin and Bow Makers* 7 vols. Brighton, 1959-1969. Henley 1961

Henley, William. *Antonio Stradivari*. Co. Woodcock, rev. and ed. Brighton, 1961. Hill, Hill, and Hill 1902

Hill, W. Henry, Arthur F. Hill, and Alfred E. Hill. *Antonio Stradivari: His Life and Work (1644-1737)*. London, 1902; reprint New York, 1963. Hill, Hill, and Hill 1931

Hill, W. Henry, Arthur F. Hill, and Alfred E. Hill. *The Violin-makers of the Guarneri Family (1626-1762)*. London, 1931. Hipkins and Gibb 1888

Hipkins, A.J., and W. Gibb (illus.). *Musical Instruments: Historic, Rare and Unique*. Edinburgh, 1888; reprint London, 1921. Hubbard 1965

Hubbard, Frank. *Three Centuries of Harpsichord-making*. Cambridge, Mass., 1965. ICMM

Thompson, Oscar, ed. *International Encyclopedia of Music and Musicians*. 10th ed. Bruce Bohle, ed. New York, 1975. Jalovec 1965

Jalovec, K. *Enzyklopädie des Geigenbaues* 2 vols. Prague, 1965. Kaiser

Kaiser, T.E. *Historic Sketches of Oshawa*. N.p., n.d. (1921?). Kallman 1960

Kallman, H. *A History of Music in Canada 1534-1914*. Toronto, 1960; reprint 1969. Kallman and Beckwith 1958

Kallman, H., and J. Beckwith. "Musical Instruments, Making of." *Encyclopedia Canadiana* VII, 214-17. Ottawa, 1958. Kallman, Potvin, and Winters 1981

Kallman, H., G. Potvin, and K. Winters, eds. *Encyclopedia of Music in Canada*. Toronto, 1981. Kinsky 1929

Kinsky, G. *History of Music in Pictures*. Leipzig, 1929; trans. New York, 1951. LeVasseur 1919

LeVasseur, Nazaire. "Musique et musiciens á Québec." La Musique Québec, 1 (1919), 1:6-9, 2:14-17. Lichtenwanger et al. 1974

Lichtenwanger, W., et al. *A Survey of Musical Instrument Collections in the United States and Canada*. Ann Arbor, Mich., 1974.

List of Canadian Patents
List of Canadian patents from the beginning of the Patent Office, June 1824 to the 31st August, 1872. Ottawa, 1882; reprint 1979. Loeser 1954

Loeser, Arthur. *Men, Women and Pianos*. New York, 1954. Mahillon 1893-1912

Mahillon, V.C. *Catalogue déscriptif et analytique du Musée instrumental du Conservatoire Royal de Musique de Bruxelles* vols. I-IV. Gand, 1893-1912. Marcuse 1964

Marcuse, Sibyl. *Musical Instruments: A Comprehensive Dictionary*. Garden City, N.J., 1964. Metropolitan Museum of Art 1903

Metropolitan Museum of Art. *Catalogue of Keyboard Instruments in the Crosby Brown Collection of Musical Instruments of All Nations*. New York, 1903. Metropolitan Museum of Art 1904

Metropolitan Museum of Art. *Catalogue of the Crosby Brown Collection of Musical Instruments of All Nations: I Europe*. New York, 1904. Michel 1963

Michel, N.E. *Historical Pianos, Harpsichords, and Clavichords*. Pico Rivera, Calif., 1963; reprint 1970. Michel 1969

Michel, N.E. *Michel's Organ Atlas*. Pico Rivera, Calif., 1969. Middleton 1934

Middleton, Jesse E. *Toronto's 100 Years*. Toronto, 1934. Milne 1930. Milne 1930

Milne, H.F. *The Reed Organ: Its Design and Construction*. London, 1930. Morgan Papers

Morgan, Henry James. Papers. National Archives of Canada, MG29D61, vol. 18. Morris 1920

Morris, W. Meredith. *British Violin Makers*. London, 1920.

New Grove Dictionary
The New Grove Dictionary of Music and Musicians 20 vols. Stanley Sadie, ed. London, Washington D.C., and Hong Kong, 1980.

New Oxford Companion
The New Oxford Companion to Music 2 vols. Arnold Denis, ed. Oxford, 1983. New York Piano Company Cat., 1881-1882

New York Piano Company. *Catalogue and Price List for 1881-82*.

Oxford Companion
Scholes, Percy A. *The Oxford Companion to Music*. London, 1945. Phillips 1957

Phillips, C.E. *The Development of Education in Canada*. Toronto, 1957. Pierce 1965

Pierce, Bob. *Pierce Piano Atlas* 6th ed. Long Beach, Calif., 1965. Pohlmann 1968

Pohlmann, E. *Laute-Theorbe-Chitarrone*. Bremen, 1968. Poidras 1928-1930

Poidras, Henri. *Critical and Documentary Dictionary of Violin Makers Old and Modern* 2 vols. Rouen, 1928-1930. Rimbault 1860

Rimbault, E.F. *The Pianoforte, its Origins, Progress and Construction*. London, 1860. Robinson 1885

Robinson, C. Blackett. *History of Toronto and County of York, Ontario*. Toronto, 1885. Rosenberg 1969

Rosenberg, N., ed. *The American System of Manufacture*. Edinburgh, 1969. Russell 1976

Russell, Loris S. "Early Canadian Sewing Machines." *Canadian Collector 2*, 5 (Sept.-Oct. 1976): 26-29. Russell 1980

Russell, Loris S. "Invention and Discovery: The Role of the Inventor in Canada and the Use of Patent Office Records." In R.A. Jarrell and N.R. Ball, eds. Science, Technology, and Canadian History (conference, Kingston, Ont., 1978) 120-130. Waterloo, Ont., 1980. Sachs 1940

Sachs, C. *The History of Musical Instruments*. New York, 1940. Strocchi 1937

Strocchi, Giuseppe. *Lintoria-Storia ed Arte ... Nuovi documenti* 3rd ed., Lugo, 1937. TD 1846-1892

Directory of the City of Toronto. 1846-1892. City of Toronto Archives and Archives of Ontario. Ure 1857

Ure, G.P. *The Handbook of Toronto*. Toronto, 1857. Vidal 1876-1878

Vidal, Antoine. *Les Instruments à archet* 3 vols. Paris, 1876-1878; reprint London, 1961. Williams Book Cat.

Williams, R.S. [Jr.] *Catalogue of Rare and Modern Books on the History of Music*. Toronto, n.d.

Williams Cat. 1862
Illustrated Catalogue of Melodeons Manufactured by R.S. Williams. Toronto, 1862.

Williams Cat. 1864
A Descriptive Catalogue of the Victoria Organs and Melodeons Manufactured by R.S.

Williams. Toronto, 1864.

Williams Cat. 1905
Catalogue No. 31 of Musical Merchandise Imported and Manufactured by the R.S. Williams & Sons Co. Limited. Toronto, 1905.

Williams Cat. 1906
Williams' Old Violin Collection. Toronto, 1906.

Williams Cat. 1908
Rare Old Violins – Williams Collection. Toronto, 1908.

Williams Cat. 1910
Catalogue of Old Violins, The R.S. Williams & Sons Co. Limited. Toronto, probably 1910.

Williams Cat. 1919
Catalogue No. 36 of Musical Merchandise, The R.S. Williams & Sons Co. Limited. Toronto, 1919.

Williams Cat. 1925
Williams Musical Instruments. Catalogue No. 40. Toronto, 1925.

Williams Cat. 1928
Catalogue No. 1 of Musical Supplies: General Musical Supplies Limited, Successors to the Wholesale Division of the R.S. Williams & Sons Co. Limited. Toronto, 1928.

Williams Pamphlet
Untitled. General Musical Supplies, Limited, Toronto, probably c. 1933. In the R.S. Williams Collection, ROM. Windeler 1977

Windeler, Janet. "Williams' old junk became museum gem." *Fugue* Toronto, 2,3 (Nov. 1977): 27-29. Winternitz 1966

Winternitz, E. *Musical Instruments of the Western World.* London, 1966. Young 1980

Young, P.T. *The Look of Music: Rare Musical Instruments 1500-1900* (exhibition catalogue). Vancouver, 1980.

123

ENDNOTES

1. Kallman 1960.
2. *Commemorative Biographical Record*, p. 46.
3. Morgan Papers, p. 8459. TD 1846 lists James Darby, teacher, dwelling at Peter Street near Queen. He was probably the master of the nearest Common School, known as the John Street School, which was in the Ward of St. George.
4. Phillips 1957, p. 150.
5. Interview with R.S. Williams, Sr., *London Free Press*, London, Ontario, September 1899, Gardiner Scrapbook.
6. *Commemorative Biographical Record*, p. 46.
7. TD 1850.
8. Morgan Papers.
9. Interview with R.S. Williams, Sr., *London Free Press*, London, Ontario, September 1899, Gardiner Scrapbook.
10. "One of the most ingenious and prolific contributors to reed organ development was Jeremiah Carhart. ...What Carhart has had many innovations to his credit, the two most important generally attributed to him were probably originated by others. ...Carhart, however, was granted United States Patent number 4912 on December 18, 1846 for the suction bellows." Gellerman 1973, p. 9.
11. *Apprenticeship in Canada*.
12. "The name melodeon has become the generic term for early keyboard reed organs with horizontal cases and single footpumped vacuum bellows, although some of the early examples had pressure bellows. ...The improved melodeon was invented in 1836." Gellerman 1973, p. 42.
13. Gardiner Scrapbook; Hamilton City Directory 1953, Corporation of Hamilton Public Library. The directory listing reads "Townsend, William, organ builder, b. 52 King Street West."
14. Interview with R.S. Williams, Sr., *London Free Press*, London, Ontario, September 1899, Gardiner Scrapbook.
15. TD 1855. Addresses were as follows: Joseph Harkness, 72 King Street West; Haycraft, Small and Addison, 1 King Street West; A. & S. Nordheimer, 14 King Street East; John Thomas & Son, 140 King Street West.
16. TD 1856. In the alphabetical listing of citizens, Richard Williams is listed: "Williams, Richard, cook and confectioner, Sayer-Street, W.S." In the same section appears the listing "Williams, R.S., melodeon manufactuer, 144 Yonge-Street, e.s." The listing in the "Professional and trades directory" section reads "Williams, L. S [sic] 144 Yonge-Street."
17. Arthur 1974, p. 119.
18. Williams Book Cat., Preface.

19. TD 1856.
20. Assessment Roll, 1857. Entry appears in the section listing Yonge Street liberties.
21. TD 1859-60. The first listing appears in the alphabetical listing of citizens.
22. TD 1861.
23. *Commemorative Biographical Record*, P. 46.
24. TD 1856.
25. *Commemorative Biographical Record*, p. 46.
26. Williams Book Cat.
27. Williams Cat. 1862, Remarks.
28. Williams Cat. 1862, Testimonials, p. 12.
29. Williams Cat. 1862, Testimonials, p. 12.
30. Williams Cat. 1862, Testimonials, p. 12.
31. Williams Cat. 1862, Testimonials.
32. Williams Cat. 1862, Testimonals.
33. The fife of these years was actually a small, high-pitched transverse flute. When this catalogue was issued by R.S. Williams the so-called modern flute had only been in use for fifteen years.
34. Thomas Simpson Cooke (1792-1848) was a composer, conductor and teacher, author of a treatise on singing. Luigi Lablanche (1794-1858) was author of *Methode de chant*.
35. Williams Cat. 1864, Introduction.
36. Williams Cat. 1864, Introduction.
37. Williams Cat. 1864, p. 6.
38. Williams Cat. 1864, p. 6..
39. Williams Cat. 1864, p. 7.
40. Williams Cat. 1864, p. 6.
41. *The Globe,* Toronto, October 12, 1863.
42. *Canadian Baptist,* October 15, 1863.
43. *Christian Guardina,* February 10, 1864.
44. *Irish Canadiian,* October 1863.
45. Williams Cat. 1864, Introduction.
46. Williams Cat. 1862, Remarks. "I combine all the improvements up to the present time."
47. Aslin 1962, p. 37. "How far reaching was the process of shaping and the public taste is well illustrated in catalogues of exhibitions such as the Great Exhibition in London in 1851, the Exhibition of 1855 in Paris, and even some of earlier date, such as the Paris Exhibition of 1844. But the Great Exhibition and its successors in Europe and the United States (e.g. the New York Exhibition of 1853) give a misleading picture of furniture in common use; the exhibits were intended for sales to wealthy people only. The Great Exhibition showed also that at this date beauty and ornament were synonymous, and embellishment was added to an existing piece of furniture or a piano, or harmonium for that matter. Thus the basic design of the exhibits was not in the contemporary style."
48. Brown's Toronto General Directory, 1859-1865. In the years 1859-1860 under "Music Sellers, &c." and under "Pianoforte tuners" is listed "Searle, Henry, 340 Yonge St."; in the calssified advertisements, Butland is introduced as "piano tuner and repairer." The number of music teachers listed under the heading "Music Professors" is four, among them "Strathy, George, W., 165 Strachan St." The piano manufacturer Thomas, after 1859, became also a dealer, with a wide assortment of pianofortes and melodeons imported from the United States.

    In the next year, 1861, the number of "Piano Makers" or "dealers" had risen to eleven, to the previous year's

125

list being added the names Burke, M.; Denning, Francis; Dingle, John; Hagar, John—Tuner; Hudson, Benjamin; Matthew, W.; and Rostraw, Andrew.

49. Brown's Toronto General Directory, 1859-1865.
50. Williams Cat. 1864, p. 24.
51. Williams Cat. 1862, Introduction.
52. Gellerman 1973, p. 12.
53. Russell, 1980, p. 27.
54. *Christian Guardian,* February 10, 1864.
55. Interview with R.S. Williams, Sr., *London Free Press*, London, Ontario, September 1899, Gardiner Scrapbook. "For ten years Mr. Williams was the exclusive maker of reed organs in this country, and he took advantage of the opportunity to make a fortune."
56. Interview with R.S. Williams, Sr., *London Free Press*, London, Ontario, September 1899, Gardiner Scrapbook.
57. TD 1856, Introduction, pp. xvii-xviii. In the same directory, under the heading "Tariff of Customs," among the duty-free articles are listed "Instruments, Musical, specially imported for use of Military Bands," another aspect of the music business in which R.S. Williams was involved.
58. Morgan Papers.
59. Morgan Papers.
60. Arthur 1974, p. 52.
61. Firth 1966, p. 168.
62. Morgan Papers.
63. Ehrlich 1976, p. 12.
64. Ehrlich 1976, p. 52.
65. *Great Exhibition*, 2:1852.
66. Ehrlich 1976, p.131.
67. Ehrlich 1976, p. 129.
68. Rosenburg 1969, p. 175.
69. Dolge 1911, p. 119.
70. Kallman 1960, p. 116.
71. *Great Exhibition*, 2:962.
72. *List of Canadian Patents*, pp. 6-220.
73. *List of Canadian Patents*, p. 10.
74. Dolge 1911, p. 446.
75. Middleton 1934, p. 79.
76. Harding 1933, p. 202.
77. Harding 1933, p. 107. Further discussion on pp. 326, 430.
78. Harding 1933, p. 296. Further discussion on pp. 347, 428.
79. Robinson 1885, p. 396. In 1885, Coleman is listed as an organ builder, trading under the name of Coleman and Sons.
80. *The Globe,* Weekly Edition, Toronto, August 10, 1866.
81. Rimbault 1860, p. 212-214.
82. Of these seventeen, the marker-off would mark out the scale, finish the beech bridge and fix its pins, insert the upward bearing bridge and bore it for the tuning pins. The finisher would assemble and fix the action, bringing the whole mechanism into playing order. The rougher-up would give the instrument its first tuning. If the tuner worked simultaneously the rougher-up could be spared. The regulator of tones and the regulator of action could also be one man. Additional operations by individual craftsmen such as the top maker, plinther, fronter, lyre maker, leg-block maker, leg maker, turner, carver, gilder, scraper, and polisher could also be combined through a reasonable division of labour.
83. Dolge 1911, p. 180.
84. *Great Exhibition*, 2:961-2.
85. Dolge 1911, pp. 63-4.
86. TD 1874. R.S. Williams' personal entry includes his addresses: "143-143 1/2 Yonge h. 166 Carlton." The other

piano builders listed were "Heintzman & Co., 117 King s; Mason, Risch & Newcombe, 81 King e; Thomas Johm 17 Buchanan." The list of "Musical instruments and music dealers" includes entries for Butland, Claxton, David, Nordheimer & Son, and Toulman. The only organ builder listed is "Dalton, Richard H., 17 Francis."

87. TD 1875.
88. Morgan Papers.
89. *Commemorative Biographical Record*, p. 349.
90. TD 1878. Robert Williams is listed at his new address at 49 Isabella Street. R.W. Williams home address is by this time "n w cor. Wellesley and Sherbourne."
91. Records of the Provincial Secretary: Business Partnership, pre-1900, November 2, 1880.
92. TD 1880. R.S. Williams is listed as a "piano and organ dealer" with a business address of 143 Yonge, and a factory at 31 Hayter. The next listing is "Williams, R.S. & Son, piano factory, 31 Hayter." In the Business Directory of the same book, in the section on "Pianos and Organs," are repeated the entries for the Williams firm at 143 Yonge and 31 Hayter Streets with the other establishments in Toronto in 1880: "Claxton Thos., 197 Yonge: Heintzman & Co., 117 King w.; Livingston J.A., 114 King w,; Mason & Risch, 32 King w.; Newcombe Octavius & Co., 107 Church; Nordheimer A. & S., 15 King e.; Norris Wm Son, 8 Adelaide e."

To complete the overview of the business, the list of "Music Dealers" of the same Directory should be added: "Billing Wm. H., 56 Agnes; Butland Richard B., 37 King w.; Claxton Thomas, Dealer in Sheet and Book Music and Musical Instruments; Bell & Co.'s Organs sold on monthly payments, 197 Yonge Street; Nordheimer A. & S., 15 King e.; Plasket J.S. 384 1/2 Yonge; Suckling I. & Sons, 107 Yonge; Williams R.S., 143 Yonge." The system of listing is peculiar, but it gives an opportunity to follow the changing situation in the number and type of firms in Toronto involved in popularizing music, and the ways in which they combined activities.

93. Morgan Papers.
94. TD 1873. In the Directories of the City of Toronto, Torrington's name appears in the list of "Music Teachers," the number of which grew from year to year. In the year of his debut in Toronto the list has twenty-two names; Torrington's address is 336 Jarvis.

A music teacher by the name "Barton, George H." lived in the "Grand Opera House Buildings, 9 Adelaide w."; the house was opened in 1874. This is documentary information about an event that indicates a different trend in the contemporary life of music in Toronto, so marked as it was with the tradition of oratorio performance. Although the function of these Grand Opera Houses was not wholly dedicated to the performance of operatic pieces, in 1880 four or five different companies entertained Torontonians.

95. New York Piano Company Cat. 1881-1882.
96. The catalogue was published for use in Canada; the head office of the company was at 226 St. James Street, Montreal, with branch houses in "Toronto, Hamilton, Ottawa, Quebec, St. John, Winnipeg, Etc."
97. Loesser 1954.
98. New York Piano Company Cat. 1881-1882.

99. New York Piano Company Cat. 1881-1882.
100. New York Piano Company Cat. 1881-1882.
101. In addition to the piano manufacturers, Canadian producers of organs are also represented. The Bell Organ in this catalogue is offered in nine styles in the "Universal Case" and seven styles in "Cabinet Case," organs in either case being identical in basic form.
102. Dolge 1911, pp. 379-381.
103. Robinson 1885, 1:397.
104. Loesser 1954, p. 527.
105. TD 1881, Business Directory. The address for the new firm was 78 Adelaide W.
106. Robinson 1885, 1:398.
107. Robinson 1885, 1:398.
108. These other quotations from Laver are frm th minute transcription of the original manuscript.
109. Robinson 1885, 1:399.
110. Arthur 1974, pp. 128, 171, 173, 174. At that time were built, for example, the Eighth Post Office on Adelaide Street (1871-1873), the A.R. McMaster and Bro. Dry Goods Warehouse at Yonge and Front Streets (1871), and the new Grand Opera House, shown in the weekly magazine *Canadian Illustrated News* in 1874. Also built in the same style was the Customs House at the corner of Front and Yonge Streets in 1876. Some sense of the style can be evinced from a description of the Grand Opera House: "The engraving of the exterior indicates a building a quite frightening scale and proportion."
111. *Commemorative Biographical Record*, p. 348.
112. Morgan Papers; Kaiser, p. 167.
113. W. Ford Lindsay, *Oshawa Times*, quoted in Kaiser, p. 167.
114. W. Ford Lindsay, *Oshawa Times*, quoted in Kaiser, p. 167.
115. Virtually all the businesses listed were located in a few square blocks centred at the corner of Yonge and King Streets.
116. Middleton 1934, p. 111.
117. Williams Book Cat.
118. Dept. of the Provincial Secretary, Charters, Liber 38, no. 31.
119. *Commemorative Biographical Record*, p. 348.
120. Sachs 1940, p. 386. "...in the 18th century, the colours had been softened, the bowed stops like the viola da gamba, vibrato effects by the tremulant or by the pulsatory vox humana turned a vibration higher or lower than the other stops were introduced in it and crescendo pedals were added in a tendency towards the expressive style of contemporary music in general."

 For more information on pipe organs, see *New Grove Dictionary*, vol. 13.
121. The Albertan, Calgary, Saturday June 8, 1968, p. 21. Clipping courtesy of Elwyn S. Davies. The description of the organ included the organ specifications; see Appendix C.
122. Bob Witham, letter to the author, c. 1984.
123. Arthur 1974, p. 187.
124. Gardiner Scrapbook.
125. Morgan Papers.
126. If the first name of the composer is an error for Edwin, then he is the composer of best-selling contemporary Canadian salon pieces and dances. Kallmann 1960, p. 257.
127. Kallmann, Potvin, and Winters 1981,

      p. 371a.
128. Kallmann 1960, p. 258.
129. Williams Cat. 1919, p. 208.
130. Kallman, Potvin and Winters 1981, pp. 665, 1002.
131. *CMTJ*, 2, No. 6 (1901):24.
132. *CMTJ*, 2, No. 6 (1901):24.
133. Department of the Provincial Secretary, Original Charters 1902, p. 69, no. 90; and *Commemorative Biographical Record*, p. 46.
134. Williams Cat. 1905.
135. Williams Cat. 1905.
136. Williams Cat. 1905.
137. Williams Cat. 1905. This violin was named after the famous Norwegian violinist, Ole Borneman (1810-1880), known as Ole Bull, who possessed the so-called Spanish Stradivari of 1687, among other precious violins. He gave concerts in Montreal in 1844, in Toronto in 1844 and 1857, and in Saint John, New Brunswick, in 1853.
138. *Commemorative Biographical Record*, p. 47.
139. Henley 1959-1969, "R.S. Williams and Sons."
140. Williams Cat. 1906. This motto was apparently borrowed from the title page of the 1885 edition of George Hart's *The Violin, Its Famous Makers and Their Imitators*. The quotation itself is from a work by W.E. Gladstone.
141. Williams Cat. 1906.
142. In the early years of the nineteenth century such trade and collecting activities had secured fame for the great pioneer connoisseur and collector Luigi Tarisio of Milan (d. 1854).
143. Williams Cat. 1906, p. 6.
144. Williams Cat. 1906, p. 6.
145. Williams Cat. 1906, p. 13.
146. Williams Cat. 1906, p. 22.
147. Williams Cat. 1906, p. 26.
148. Williams Cat. 1906, pp. 30-32.
149. Williams Cat. 1906, pp. 9, 18.
150. Williams Cat. 1906, p. 9.
151. Williams Cat. 1908, p. 23.
152. Williams Cat. 1908, p. 24.
153. Williams Cat. 1908, p. 25. This was aneminent firm of violin makers and experts founded about 1825 by the father of George Hart the violinist.
154. Williams Cat. 1908, p. 26.
155. Williams Cat. 1908, p. 32.
156. Williams Cat. 1908, p. 34.
157. Williams Cat. 1908, p. 36.
158. Williams Cat. 1908, 1910. The writer is assumed to be Karl Ondricek, a violinist mentioned as a member of the Kneisel Quartet in Boston, who perhaps later moved to New York; however, he never taught the famous Czech violin virtuoso Jan Kubelik. *Grove Dictionary* vol. 1; *Oxford Companion*, p. 971.
159. "Two Amatis," *Toronto World*, May 1, 1910.
160. Of these four makers only Joseph Hugil is included in *Henley's Universal Dictionary of Violin and Bow Makers*. Hugil was born in Wales about 1838, and in his early years emigrated to Canada, settling in Ontario. After establishing a repair shop in Toronto, he produced more than two hundred instruments. One of his violins was accepted by Ysaye. He died in 1910, just about the time this catalogue was issued.
161. "Canadian Has World-Wide Reputation as Violin Expert," *Toronto World*, May 1, 1910.
162. "Canadian Has Worl-Wide Reputation as Violin Expert," *Toronto World*, May

1, 1910.

163. "Gift to Elman," *Toronto World*, May 1, 1910.

164. "Two Amatis," *Toronto World*, May 1, 1910.

165. It is known that Mr. John Loudon in 1901-1902 played the viola in the Klingenfeld String Quartette organized by Heinrich Klingenfeld, then music teacher in the Metropolitan School of Music and Toronto Conservatory of Music. Kallmann 1960, p. 501.

166. Sevcik letter to R.S. Williams, August 9, 1911.

167. *Canadian Journal of Music,* May 1914.

168. *CMTJ*, 15, No. 9 (1915): 56.

169. *CMTJ*, 15, No. 9 (1915):56.

170. Williams Cat. 1906.

171. *CMTJ*, 15, No. 9 (1915):56.

172. *CMTJ*, 25, No. 6:38-41.

173. *CMTJ*, 14, No. 4 (1913):43

174. "On account of the narrow width of the lot and the city Building By-law limiting the height of a building to five times its width, it was necessary to keep the floor heights as low as possible. They were limited for most floor to 10 ft. 8 in. ...The building was designed by Messrs. Chapman & McGriffin, architects, and erected by Messrs. Jago & Harris, general contractors."

"The New Williams Building, Toronto," *Contract Record*, November 27, 1912. (Courtesy of Municipal Library, City Hall, Toronto.)

175. *CMTJ*, 13, No. 8 (1913):47.

176. *CMTJ,* 13 No. 9 (1913):30-31.

177. *CMTJ*, 13, No. 9 (1913):30-31.

178. *CMTJ*, 13, No. 9 (1913):30-31.

179. "Twenty-three years after," *CMTJ*, 14, No. 3(1913):101.

180. *CMTJ*, 14, No. 1 (1913):59.

181. *CMTJ*, 14, No. 3 (1913):79. The statement that the collection was *loaned* is incorrect.

182. Janet Windeler, "Williams' Old Junk Became Museum Gem," *Fugue*, 2, No. 3 (1977).

183. R.S. Williams Collection, ROM.

184. First published by Ladislav Cselenyi in "The Mirror of Music in the ROM", *Rotunda*, 5, No. 3 (Summer 1972):18-20.

185. Williams Book Cat., Preface.

186. Henley 1959-1969, vol. 1. Ardern's violins are not mentioned in the Williams catalogues.

187. *Canadian Journal of Music*, July-August 1914.

188. *CMTJ*, January 1916, Export Trade Section.

189. *Canadian Journal of Music,* March 1916, p.206.

190. *Canadian Journal of Music,* March 1916, p. 206.

191. Henley 1961, entry on the 1683 Stradivari violin.

192. *AMB*. All of this took place at a time when the application of scientific methods to such objects was only beginning; today the results are accessible to dealers, buyers, collectors, artists, museums, etc. and are used in combination with the old method of evaluation by intuition.

193. *Commemorative Biographical Record*, in an article on R.S. Williams, Jr., p. 348.

194. "Is a Jew's Harp a musical instrument?" (Unsigned), *CMTJ*, 13, No. 10 (1913):63.

195. "Interviewed Mr. Edison. Mr. R.S. Williams and Department Managers Visit Edison Plant." (Unsigned), *CMTJ*, 14, No. 8 (1914):55.

196. *CMTJ*, 17, No. 2:57.

197. This phonograph was sent to the Sombra Township Museum in 1961.
198. *CMTJ,* 15, No. 1(1914):48.
199. Ehrlich 1976, p. 169.
200. *CMTJ,* 15, No. 1:59.
201. *CMTJ,* 16, No. 8:55.
202. "Williams Pianos sent to all parts of the world," *The Oshawa Daily Reformer,* June 30, 1927.
203. *CMTJ,* (Feb. 1919):78.
204. William Book Cat. This is all that is known about Dulunet.
205. Henley 1959-1969, 2:43-44.
206. Williams Book Cat. Preface.
207. Henley 1959-1969, 2:43-44.
208. Henley 1959-1969, 2:43-44.
209. Williams Cat. 1925, p. 137.
210. Williams Book Cat.
211. R.S. Williams Collection, ROM.
212. R.S. Williams Collection, ROM. The earliest known English square pianoforte of normal construction is that made by Johann Zumpe in 1767. *Victoria and Albert Museum, Catalogue of Music Instruments,* vol. 1, Key Instruments. London, 1968, p.60.
213. *CMTJ,* 25, No. 6 (1924):39-40.
214. Department of Consumer & Commercial Relations, Corporate Name Search.
215. *The Globe,* Toronto, September 27, 1928.
216. *The Globe,* Toronto, September 27, 1928.
217. *The Globe,* Toronto, September 27, 1928.
218. *Mail and Empire,* Toronto, October 27, 1928.
219. R.S. Williams & Son Co. Ltd., April 1, 1931, Rec. group 55, Chart Book 278, Fol. 44 1-2-B, Ontario Archives.
220. Ontario Archives, Liber 228, recorded as No. 30.
221. Jo Aldwinckle, "Major industry to rubble," *This Week,* Oshawa, November 4, 1970, P. 14. At this time, of course, there was no Williams involved in the Oshawa business; it is to the company that the article refers.

    The three years mentioned are probably the years after 1927, because in an interview with Mr. Carlyle, the vice-president of the Williams Piano Company, which appeared in the *Oshawa Daily Reformer* of June 30, 1927, there was no mention of the production of radios in a lengthy discucssion about the "improving" piano business.
222. Jo Aldwinckle, "Major industry to rubble," *This Week,* Oshawa, November 4, 1970, p. 14.
223. Isobel Brock, interview with the author, summer 1974.
224. William Cat. 1928, p. 151
225. Williams Cat. 1928, p. 152.
226. Williams Pamphlet.
227. Williams Pamphlet.
228. Archives, ROM.
229. Archives, ROM.
230. Archives, ROM.
231. R.S. Williams Collection, ROM.
232. Williams Book Cat.
233. Obituary by Fred Davy, *Telegram,* Toronto, March 31, 1945.
234. *CMTJ,* 18, No. 4 (September 19170: 41, 43.
235. Jo Aldwinckle, "Major industry to rubble," *This Week,* Oshawa, November 4, 1970, p. 14.

INDEX

A
A&S Nordheimer, 14
Adams, William, 96
Agricultural and Arts Association Exhibition (1870), 17
Agricultural Association of Upper Canada, 17
Aid, Loan and Saving Company, 61
Albert, (Bow-maker), 73
Allin, Mr., 19
Amati, Nicholas, 70, 77
Amsterdam, 74
"Andreas Guarnerius", 69
Andrus Brothers, 29
Antonio Stradivari, his life & work, 91
Arden, Job, 89
Arne, Dr. Thomas Augustine, 99
Arnold, Samuel, 109
Attwood, Thomas, 108
Austin, Charles C., 27
Australia, 96
Awde, Robert, 61
Aylesford, Lord (Earl of Aylesford), 90, 91, 104

B
Baird, W.M., 38
Baltimore, Maryland, 17
Bancroft, Marshall S., 38
Banister, John, 109
Banks, Benjamin, 75
Bartram, Mr., 52
Bayley, John, 40
Beethoven, Ludwig van, 108
Belgium, 41
Bell, Daniel, 38
Berini, S., 97
Berlin, 21, 69
Berlioz, Hector, 108
Bernardel, (Bow-maker), 73
Bertilotti, Gasparo da Salo, 70, 77, 78
Betts, John, 75
Birdsall, Thomas, 86

Boston, (Mass), 10, 25, 27, 42
Bouckley, Thomas, 50, 57, 58, 59, 64, 65, 83, 100
Brampton, (ON), 46
Bridge, Sir John Frederick, 108
Brighton (ON), 49
Britain, 20, 34, 37
Brock (ON.), 20
Brock, Mrs. Isobel W., 16, 19, 39, 46, 47, 53, 60, 65, 66, 68, 73, 77, 104, 109, 111
Brock, Lieutenant Governor, 30
Brown, John, 88
Buffalo (N.Y.), 19, 27
Bull, Frederick, 68, 82
Burlington, (ON), 58
Burney, Dr. Charles, 107
Burt, George, 82
Butland, Richard B., 26

C
Calgary, (Sask.), 53, 54, 85, 88, 95
Campbell, John Douglas, Marquis of Lorne, 61
Canada West, 29, 35
Canadian Bandsman and Musician, 66
Canadian Bandsman and Orchestra Journal, 66
Canadian Journal of Music, 90, 91
Canadian Music and Trade Journal, 66, 79, 81, 85, 87, 91, 94
Canadian National Exhibition, 82, 94, 101
Canadian Patent Office, 28
Canadian Organ and Piano Co., 32, 38, 39
Canadian Vitaphone Company, 93
Careno, Teresa, 83
Carhart and Needham, 26
Carhart's Melodeon Instructor, 41
Carhart, Jeremiah, 12
Casals, Pablo, 104

Catalogue of Rare and Modern Books on the History of Music, 89
Cayuga, (ON), 56, 57, 59
Cayuga, 95
Cerute, (sic) Giovanni Battista, 74
Chanot, François, 73, 74
Chappuy, Nicholas Augustin, 74
Chickering of Boston, 33
China, 96
Chippewa (steamer), 87
Church of the Children of Peace, 10
Christian Guardian, 28
Christophori, Bartolommeo, 32
Civil War (American War), 29, 33
Clarin, Charles, 95
Clarke, James P., 40
Clayton, H.Y., 92
Coates, Richard, 10
Cockburn, H.D., 86
Coleman;
    Alma, (Mrs. R.S. Williams Jr.), 53
    Charles (C.R.), 53, 86, 95
    James, 36
Collection of Hart & Son, 75
Columbia Records of Canada, 93
Concord, New Hampshire, 12, 27
Confederation, 40
Connoly, Joseph, 55
Covent Garden Theatre, 108
Corelli, Archangelo, 99
Coutourie, Mr., 66
Craske, George, 73, 75
Croden, John A., 52, 86, 87
Crotch, Williams, 108
Currelly, Dr. C.T., 88, 89, 99, 105, 106
Czerny, Karl, 108

D
Dalton (Toronto), 29
Daniel Bell Organ Co., 45
Darby, Mr., (James), 11
Debain, Alexandre, 25
Decker & Son (New York), 41, 42, 43

De Forest-Crossley, 103
Delivet, Auguste, 97, 98, 99, 101, 104
Denis, (Violin-maker), 73
Derazey, H., 74
Dies, George E., 82
Didier, Nicholas, 72, 74
Dinsmore, John I., 86, 95
Disk Talking Machine Co. (The), 93
Dodd, (Violin-maker), 90
Donizetti, Gaetano, 108
Dragonetti, Domenico, 78, 99, 108
Dubay Organs Ltd. (Burlington), 58
Dublin, 75
Duke of Leinster, 78
Duke, Richard, 73, 75
Dulunet, Mr., 97

E
Earle of Aylesford Stradivari, 90, 104
Eberle, Udalricus Johannes, 73
Edinburgh, 75
Edison Concert, 94
Edison Dealer's Convention, 93
Edison Diamond Disc, 94
Edison, (phonograph), 69, 86, 92, 93, 94
Edison, (Thomas Alva), 93, 94, 109
Elsler, Johann, Joseph, 75
Elman, Mischa, 77, 78, 104
England, 9, 32, 41, 52, 68, 81, 88, 95, 99, 101, 107
Ennis & Co., 83, 84
Estey of Brattleboro (Vermont), 24, 25

F
First General Common School Act of Canada (1840), 11
Fisher, Arthur Elwell ("Dr."), 40, 50, 51
Fisher, Edward, 40, 51
Fitch, Eby and Thwaite, 39
Flotow, Freidrich, 108
Ford, Jeffrey, 86, 92
Fortong, John, 76
Freiburg, (Germany), 32
France, 32, 41, 81
"Francesco Ruggeri" (sic), 69, 72, 73
Friederici, Christian Ernst, 32

G
Gardini (sic) [Felice de Giardini], 90, 91
George A. Prince (Buffalo), 27
General Musical Supplies Ltd., 103, 104, 105
Geneva, 91
Germany, 32, 41, 81
"Giovan Grancino", 69

Glasgow, 95
Glass, Johann, 69, 70, 73, 75
Gledhill, Edward, 61
Globe and Mail, 111
Gloor, Elizabeth, 91
Goddard, Arabella, 108
Godley, William, 76
Goold, Mr., 109
Gounod, Charles, 108
Grammar School, 19
Grand Trunk Railway, 29, 88
Grant, Barefoot & Co., 45
Great Exhibition (London) 1851, 34, 38
Grisi, Giulia, 108
Guarneri [Gurneri (sic)], Pietro, 70, 74, 110

H
H&J Philips (Halifax), 34
Hale, Joseph P., 35, 37, 38, 41, 42, 43, 44
Halevy, Jacques, Fromental, 108
Halifax, 10, 34
Hall Company, 49
Hall, John, 26
Hall, Marie, 79
Hamilton (ON), 10, 12, 13, 14, 16, 83, 87
Hamilton Daily Spectator and Journal of Commerce, 34
Hamlin, Emmons, 27, 28
Handel, George Frideric, 108, 109
Harding, R.E., 35
Harris, Reverend Richard H., 20
Hart, George, 109
Hart, Herbert, 109
Harvey, Lieutenant Governor Sir John, 34
Hassall, J.A., 96
Hawkins History of Music, 99
Haycroft, Small & Addison, 14
Heinl, George, 88, 97
Heintzman & Co. (Toronto), 42, 43, 45
Heintzman (Heintzmann), Theodore August, 42
Henley, William, 91
Herbret, John W., 34, 37, 38
Her Majesty, The Queen, 63
Hill, A. Phillips, 109, 110
Hill, Arthur F., 89, 99, 109
Hill, Charles, 109
Holland, 4
Holmes, William, 108
Hood, T.D. 34
Hopt, J., 70
Hugil, Joseph, 76
Hund, Frederick, 10

Hunter, Mr., 90

I
Isle of Wight, 20, 36
Italy, 32

J
J.L. Orme & Son, 66
Jais, Anton, 73
Jamaica, 95
Japan, 96
Jarvis Collegiate Institute, 48
John Thomas & Son, 14, 34, 35
Joseph Hall Machine Works, 50
Joseph Harkness (Co.), 14

K
Kleymans, Cornelius, 74
Klotz, Joseph, 70, 73
Kingston (ON), 14, 23
Kneizel, August, 69
Kneizel Quartette, 76
Kney, Gabriel, 56
Kreisler, Fritz, 97, 104
Kubelik, Jan, 76, 79

L
Labitzky, W., 19
Lablanche, Luigi, 21
Lambert, J.N., 73, 74
Laurilliard, A., 34
Lavallée, Augustin, 76
Laver, Jim, 45, 46, 47, 50
Leipzig, 69, 70, 75
le Jeune, Claude, 107, 109
Leschetizsky, Theodor, 108
Letter Envelope Company Ltd., 75
Lind, Jenny, 15, 108
London, (ON), 29, 45, 51, 56, 59
London (U.K.), 10, 32, 68, 70, 73, 75, 81, 88, 89, 95, 97, 99, 109
London Free Press, 14, 29, 59
Low, Thomas, 109
Lowendall, Louis, 69
Lower Canada, 34
Loudon, John S., 76, 79, 81, 90
Lucas, Charles, 108
Lunenburg (Nova Scotia), 76
Lyonais, Pierre Olivier, 10, 76

M
Maggini, G.P., 70
Mahon, Edward, 30
Majestic electric radio, 102
Malay States, 96
Malibran, Marie F., 108
Manchester, 75
Mandy, Arthur, 86

133

Manley, Morris, 64
Mario, Giovanni, 108
Maritimes, 62
Mason & Hamlin, 24, 25, 26
Massey Hall, 51, 77, 83, 94
Massey, Hart, A., 51
Matthew Hardy & Son, 75
Matushek, Frederick, 33
Maver, George, 16
Mazas, Jacques-Féréol, 21
Melba, Mme., 82
McCarroll, J., 19
McCaul, Reverend John, 40
McGee, James, 38
McLean, William, 38
McPhillips, Wm., 52
Meade, G.W., 10
Meade, George Hooper, 34, 35
Mendelssohn-Bartholdy, F., 108
Mendelssohn Choir, 51
Metropolitan Choral Society, 15
Metropolitan Toronto Library Board, 63
Michel's Organ Atlas, 12
Middleton, William, 87
Midland (ON), 55, 59, 63
Might, John M., 38
Miller, John M., 38
Milligan, George, 34
Mirecourt, 73
Mittenwald, 73
Model School, 15, 17, 19
Montreal, 29, 34, 35, 37, 42, 43, 82, 85, 86, 95
Morris, Mr. (grocer), 50
Morris, William, 30, 31
Moore;
  Dr. William, 39, 51
  William Elwood, 51, 68
Mount Pleasant Cemetery, 110, 111
Mudie, Thomas, 108
Muir, Alexander, 64
Munro, Mr. (Head Customs Officer), 52
Musical Courier, 27

N
National Gallery, 61
National Library of Canada, 9, 42, 43, 52, 54, 63, 67, 84, 85, 86, 93, 96
Newell, Augustus, 45, 49
Newell Organ Reed Co., 45
New Hampshire (U.S.), 12
Newmarket (ON), 16
Newton, John, 82
New York, 33, 35, 43, 44
New York Piano Company, 41, 42, 43, 44, 45

New Zealand, 95
Niagara Falls (ON), 87
Normal School, 15, 19
Nordheimer;
  Abraham, 14
  Samuel, 14
Nordheimer Piano & Music Co. Ltd., 49, 50
Norris;
  Mary DeMain, 13
  Robert, 13
  Sarah DeMain, 13, 16, 30, 38, 39, 61, 101, 111
Northern Railway, 16
Nova Scotia, 34, 76
Nurnburger, (Bow-maker), 73

O
O'Connor, James, 82
O'Neil (Toronto), 29
Ontario
  Oshawa (ON), 19, 49, 50, 53, 54, 57, 58, 59, 63, 64, 65, 68, 70, 83, 95, 99, 100, 103, 104, 111
  Oshawa Manufacturing Co. (Oshawa Piano Works), 49, 65
Ondricek, K., 76
Orpheus Britannicus, 109
Ottawa, 9, 66, 68
Owen, Richard, 34
Owen Sound Registered Music Teachers' Association, 64

P
Paderewski, Ignace, 108
Paganini, Nicola (sic), 74, 108
Paris, 25, 69, 70, 75, 81, 95, 97
Paris Exhibition (1867), 32
Parker, Daniel, 75
Pathé Records and Pathephone Agency, 93
Perry, Thomas, 75
Petch, Glen B., 86, 92
Peterborough Central Exhibition (1888), 17
Phoenix Foundry, 37
Postachini, Andrea, 72
Prague, 73, 79
Pratt, Mrs. Charles Edward, 98
Pratt of Winchester, New Hampshire, 27
Press, (Violin virtuoso), 104
Preston, (ON), 51
Prince Edward Island (PEI), 46
Prince, George, A., 27, 28
Prince & Smith's, 19, 26
Princess Louise, 61
Provincial Agricultural Association

of Upper Canada (1863), 24
Provincial Exhibition (1863), 23
Provincial and Agricultural Exhibition (1865), 17
Purcell, Henri, 108

Q
Quebec, 10, 29, 34, 43, 66
Queenston Heights (ON), 95

R
R.S. Williams Building, 84, 111
R.S. Williams Co., 19
R.S. Williams Collection, 9, 12, 62, 69, 73, 74, 75, 85, 88, 106
R.S. Williams House, 52, 82, 85
R.S. Williams & Sons Co., 30, 37, 40, 41, 43, 44, 45, 47, 50, 51, 62, 68, 83, 85, 86, 87, 88, 90, 92, 95, 96
R.S. Williams & Sons Co. Ltd., 53, 54, 55, 56, 61, 62, 64, 65, 66, 71, 88, 92, 98, 99, 101, 103, 104, 105
Reciprocity Treaty (1854), 29
Remenyi House of Music, 71, 72, 99
Remenyi, Michael, 9, 99
Robertson, Alexander L., 66, 105
Rogers, 102
Rogers-Majestic, 103
Romberg, Bernard, 21
Roome, T.F., 29
Ross, Hon. G.W., 63
Rottenberg, Louis, 79
Royal Academy of Music, 108
Royal Canadian Academy of Arts, 61
Royal Ontario Museum (ROM), 9, 12, 17, 36, 62, 74, 75, 77, 80, 88, 89, 94, 95, 98, 99, 105, 109, 110
Royal Society of Canada, 61
Rubenstein, Anton Gregor, 108
Rubus, Riggart, 70

S
Salisbury, 75
Sarnia (ON), 29
Sartory, Eugene, 75, 81
Scarlatti, D., 109
Schumann, Clara, 108
Sefton, H.F., 19
Sevcik, Otokar, 79, 80, 81
Scythes, E.C., 82
Shelton, F., 86
Shudi, B., 32
Sharon, (ON), 10
Silbermann, Gottfried, 32
Singapore, 96
Slatter, Lieutenant John, 65, 66
Smith, Alexander, 34, 35
Smith Brothers of Boston, 27

South America, 95
Spohr, Louis, 21
Steinway & Sons, 33, 44
St. Hyacinthe, 76
St. John's Anglican Church
   (Cayuga), 56, 57
St. Lawrence Hall, 15
St. Margaret's Roman Catholic
   Church (Midland), 54, 55
St. Mary's Catholic Church
   (Toronto), 55
St. Paul's Roman Catholic Church
   (Toronto), 55, 56, 59
St. Petersburg, 70
Saint John, 34
Stainer, J., 70
Stanton, H.G., 52, 86, 87, 88, 95
Statute of Artificers, 12
Stradivari, Antonio, 70, 91
Sunday World, 79
Suppé, Franz von, 108
Switzerland, 41

T
T.F. Roome's Organ Manufactory, 26
Tarisio, Luigi, 76
Tartini, G., 109
The Cabinet Maker's Assistant, 26
The Globe (Toronto), 23, 24, 102
Thibaud, (Violinist), 104
Thomas, Charles, L., 35
Thomas, John Morgan, 10, 34, 35
Thwaite;
   Mazo, 39, 47, 101
   Metcalf, 39, 40
Toronto College of Music, 51
Toronto Conservatory of Music, 51
Toronto Philharmonic Society, 15,
   40, 53
Toronto Star, 95
Toronto Symphony Orchestra, 77,
   83, 86
Toronto Vocal Musical Society, 15
Toronto World, 76, 77, 78
Torrington, Frederick H., 40, 51,62
Tourte, François, 70, 90
Tourte, Le Pére, 70
Townsend, William, 12, 13, 27, 28, 99
Trautenwein, 21
Trestrail, B.A., 87, 92, 102
Trestrail, F.A., 102
Trinidad, 95
Trinity College, 15
Tubbs, E.W., 73
Tupper, Rt. Hon. Sir Chas., 63

U
Union Exhibition (1864), 17

United States, 9, 13, 24, 28, 29, 31, 33,
   34, 35, 37, 38, 43, 79, 81, 85, 89
Upper Canada, 18, 62
Upper Canada College, 30

V
Vautrin, Joseph, 97
Verdi, Guiseppe, 108
Vet, C.M., 64
Victoria Organ, 22, 23, 24, 25, 26, 28
Victor Talking Machines, 93
Vienna, 69
Vigneron, (Bow-maker), 73
Vogt, Augustus Stephen, 51
Voight, Johann Georg, 75
von Giltry, Lidus, 91
von Kunits, Harriette, 79
von Kunits, Luigi, 79, 81, 90
Vose & Sons (Boston), 41, 42, 43
Vuillaume, J.B., 74, 77

W
W.E. Hill & Sons (London), 70, 73,
   75, 78, 81, 88, 90, 91, 97, 99, 109
Wagner, O., 95, 108
Wagner, Zeidler & Co., 44
Ward of St. James, 16
Ware, George, 90, 91
Warren, Samuel R., 34, 35
Waters of New York, 27
Weber, Albert, 41, 42, 43
Webster and Horsefall of
   Birmingham, 34
Wellesley Street Pubic School, 48
Welsman, Frank S., 83
Weichold, (Bow-maker), 73
Weiss, Jacob, 75
Wessel, Nickel & Gross (New York),
   44
White, Mr., 86
Western Fair (1899), 59
Wieniawski, Henri, 71
Williams;
   Alma (Mrs. Richard Sugden Jr.),
      53, 61, 88, 93
   Anne (Anna, Annie) (Mrs. Dr.
      Moore), 17, 38, 39, 51
   Frank, 17, 111
   George Arthur, 47, 51, 65, 68
   Harold Ernest, 51, 68
   Herbert DeMain, 39, 47, 52, 60,
      66, 68
   Henrietta, 17, 111
   Irma, 61, 66, 68
   Isobel (Mrs. I.W. Brock), 16, 19,
      39, 46, 47, 53, 60, 65, 66, 68,
      73, 77, 104, 109, 111
   Jane, 10, 12, 17

   Mabel, 51, 68
   Madeline, 66, 68
   Mazo (Thwaite) (Mrs. Robert
      Williams), 39, 47, 101
   Richard, 10, 14
   Richard (infant), 30, 111
   Richard Sugden Jr., 9, 16, 21, 38,
      39, 41, 46, 47, 48, 49, 53, 61,
      63, 66, 68, 69, 71, 72, 74, 76,
      77, 79, 80, 81, 86, 87, 88, 89,
      90, 91, 92, 95, 97, 98, 99, 101,
      102, 104, 105, 106, 109, 110, 111
   Richard Sugden Sr., 9, 10, 11, 12,
      13, 14, 15, 16, 17, 18, 19, 20,
      21, 22, 24, 25, 26, 27, 28, 29,
      30, 31, 32, 33, 34, 35, 36, 37,
      38, 39, 40, 42, 44, 45, 46, 49,
      50, 51, 52, 53, 60, 61, 62, 64,
      65, 68, 70, 71, 73, 74, 82, 85,
      87, 100, 101, 102, 103, 111
   Richard Sugden III, (Dick), 88
   Robert, 13, 17, 30, 31, 38, 39, 40,
      44, 47, 49, 52, 61, 65, 68, 82,
      100, 111
   Robert (great grandson), 20
   Sarah DeMain, (Norris), (Mrs.
      Richard Sugden Sr.), 13, 16,
      30, 38, 39, 61, 101, 111
   William, 38
   William Hodgson, 10, 17
Williams Musical Library, 61, 62, 64
Williams Old Violin Collection, 80
Williams Piano Company Limited,
   59, 61, 64, 68
Willis & Co., 66
Windsor, 47
Windsor Castle, 63
Winnipeg, 68, 82, 85, 88, 95, 103, 104
Witham, Bob, 55
Wittich, (song writer), 64
World War I, 95, 96, 101
Wurlitzer, 86, 102

Y
Yonge Street, 15, 31, 39, 45, 46, 47,
   52, 69, 83, 84, 85, 95, 103, 104, 111
Yule, J.L., 64

Z
Zeidler, Carl, 44
Zickel, H.H., 64
Zumpe, Johannes Christoph, 32, 99

ABOUT THE AUTHOR

Ladislav Cselenyi-Granch was born in Czechoslovakia in 1920 and served as director of the Slovak National Museum, before emigrating to Canada with his family in 1966. Now retired from his position as Curator of Musical Instruments at the Royal Ontario Museum, he is the author of several historical novels and a specialist in Central European culture.

As both an art historian and composer, he holds degrees in art history and music pedagogy from the University of J. A. Komensky, Bratislava, Czechoslovakia and the University of Toronto.